A Contemporary Social Spirituality

FRANCIS X. MEEHAN

ORBIS BOOKS
Maryknoll, New York 10545

The Catholic Foreign Mission Society of America (Maryknoll) recruits and trains people for overseas missionary service. Through Orbis Books Maryknoll aims to foster the international dialogue that is essential to mission. The books published, however, reflect the opinions of their authors and are not meant to represent the official position of the society.

Manuscript editor: Lisa McGaw

Library of Congress Cataloging in Publication Data

Meehan, Francis Xavier.
  A contemporary social spirituality.

  Bibliography: p.
  1. Spiritual life—Catholic authors.
2. Church and social problems—Catholic Church.
I. Title.
BX2350.2.M414   261.8   82-2253
ISBN 0-88344-022-9 (pbk.)   AACR2

Contents

Preface

In each area of moral theology and spirituality covered in the following chapters, I have attempted to give a fresh social perspective. In so doing I have tried to assure not only a social vision of each individual question considered, but to root the development of these questions into mainstream church teachings as well as to show their relationship to basic theology. If there is one need of those who live and work among the poor—and this book is written from the perspective of those whose work is among the poor—it is the sense of God's abiding presence with them, of God's working with them, ahead of them, and behind them. All is grace. To lose this spiritual sensitivity in one's work is to risk becoming, in Thomas Merton's phrase, a "beast of burden."

For helping to keep me from becoming a beast of burden in the work of this book I give thanks, from my heart, to family and friends for their support; to two priest blood brothers who gave me insight into particular subjects; to spiritual brothers and sisters who minister on Philadelphia streets and who provided inspiration; to the "Seminarians for Life" at St. Charles Seminary, who know a wide vision of what pro-life work is; to the St. Charles Seminary library staff, who helped me beyond the call of duty; to Sister Peggy Conry, Mrs. Kathy Kelley, Mrs. Helen McCormick, and Mrs. Peggy Burke, who generously gave time to typing and retyping.

Acknowledgments

Most of the chapters in this book appeared originally, in somewhat different form, in the following publications. Grateful acknowledgment is made for permission to use the material here.

America, for "Social Justice and Abortion"; "The Arms Race and the American Parish"; "Disarmament in the Real World."

Catholic Mind, for "The Catholic Conscience Faces the Military Draft."

Catholic Mind, and Pope John Center publication *Human Sexuality and Personhood,* for "Making the Connection between Sexual Ethics and Social Justice."

Emmanuel, for "Global Awareness: A Spirituality for Worshiping in Spirit and Truth"; "Bread-breaking and a Pastoral Care of the Milieu"; "Pope John Paul II and Social Concern"; "Eucharist and a Spirituality for Justice"; "Worship in Spirit and Truth—And Civil Religion."

The Priest, for "Why Do Social Teachings Have Little Impact? A Reflection."

Review for Religious, for "Ministry in the Church and Structural Concern for Justice."

Prologue: The Meaning of a New Social Spirituality

"Spirituality" is a difficult word to define. Yet it can be grasped simply. What Augustine said of "time" is true also of spirituality: "If no one asks me, I know; if I wish to explain it to one that asketh, I know not."[1]

To define "spirituality" with systematic comprehension is beyond the interest of this book. Formal works on the theology of the spiritual life speak of spirituality as a way of responding to God, a style of living the life of the Holy Spirit. In the history of the church, there have been many ways and many emphases on how to live the Way of life. Naturally there developed in history some varying spiritual trends and diverse accents in the awareness of a spiritual people. Sometimes these coalesced into a school of spirituality and then flowed over into the whole church. Think, for example, of Ignatius's insight into the value of apostolic activity, how it shifted the church away from seeing monastic prayer as the predominant model for spiritual living. Or consider Vincent de Paul's vision of the woman religious, how this vision slowly came to allow for the active commitment of women outside a contemplative enclosure.

The Movement toward the Social

In this book I am talking of a similar broad shift in spirituality, one that tilts spiritual living toward social concerns. Certain striking aspects make this a genuinely new phenomenon. But it is important to understand aright the word "new." I do not mean a sudden shift, as though it were something that arose only in the 1960s. Rather, it is something writ larger in historical terms, a glacierlike movement evolving over at least this entire century, gradually taking hold of whole sectors of the church. It is a calm

1

and gradual evolution, more like a steady rain of grace seeping slowly into the church's soil.

The evolution is not always perfectly linear. It surely has moments of neglect and contradiction in the church. Yet its steady, slow progress is in itself an authentication carrying something of a divine impetus.

New Yet Ancient

Here at the very beginning I wish to affirm that the social movement among spiritual people is not merely a fad, but a maturing consciousness of what it means to be a spiritual person. In this sense it is not a *new* movement. The present consciousness is a ripening of something that began toward the middle of the nineteenth century. This is what is meant by the word "new," a broad historical articulation of a phenomenon developing since the latter part of the Enlightenment.

A further caution in speaking of a social spirituality as new is the need to recognize the authentic roots of a Christian tradition that encompassed the social. In this sense new spiritual developments are never totally new. The gift of Jesus as revelation of the Father, as revelation of full humanity means that spiritual gifts in history are somehow always an unfolding of what is already given in the Lord Jesus, and in the privileged witness of the apostolic community. Authentic developments always hark back to the gospel.

What could be more clear than Jesus' own integral care for people (which we could also call a social care)? Nothing summed up Jesus' life more succinctly than his own great parable of the kingdom in Matthew's twenty-fifth chapter. Here he tells us straight out that bread given to the hungry is given to him, that water given to the thirsty is given to him. Indeed, the apostolic church summarized its insight into Jesus as the One who fulfilled the prophecy of Isaiah: "The spirit of the Lord is upon me; therefore he has anointed me. He has sent me to bring glad tidings to the poor, to proclaim liberty to the captives, recovery of sight to the blind and release to the prisoners, to announce a year of favor from the Lord" (Lk. 4:18–19).

Today's social spiritual movement is thus not seen here as an abrupt change in Christian understanding. It is something rooted in the Hebrew prophets and in him who fulfills the prophets. In the history of the church itself, one can hardly find a saint who has not given clear witness to a social overflow of his or her spiritual living. By their lives saints have taught us that every spirituality is social. Stories of lepers' sores kissed, of poor children taught, of hospitals founded—these fill the pages of the lives of the saints. Social concern is old and new.

Accenting the New Dimensions

The church's present movement can be compared to a great ship making its turn slowly in the waters of history. The turn is never swift, nor does it occur with ease. There is always the rumbling, the shuddering from within the bowels of the ship. So in the church there are the inevitable polemics, the difficulties of articulation, the theological ferment, some polarization and even mistakes. Putting one's finger on exactly what is new could fill a theological tome. For now let us merely single out some directions by which the Spirit seems to be guiding the turning ship of Peter.

First of all and most simply, there is in the twentieth century a new consciousness that many see as a post-Enlightenment consciousness. It is an awareness that we are agents of history rather than spectators. People sense within themselves that they need not merely undergo history, but that they can participate. This shift in consciousness is in some ways a new humanity, an anthropological breakthrough. It does not mean that post-Enlightenment men or women are better than their forebears, just different. It is a different self-consciousness from that of "feudal man." Take the term "social justice." Such a concept as we know it today was hardly imagined before the eighteenth century. Naturally Christian men and women knew that holiness implied justice between individuals, between rulers and subjects; and naturally they knew somehow that spiritual living precluded acts of greed or unfair exchange. But what they could not have realized, as we do today, is how greed could become embodied within the very structures of a society. This was a thought whose time had largely to await the nineteenth century.

Leo XIII's *Rerum Novarum,* written in 1891, was a milestone indicating that the church was irrevocably casting a new mold for the spirituality of the future. Even though some of Leo's thought was still rooted in hierarchical society, he made a quantum leap in his empathetic response to the insight of the sociologists who had written before him. Once and for all it becomes recognized that justice involves something more than one individual's goodwill. Now it is seen also as something that should be basic to the patterns of human organization. This concept becomes even clearer in the writings of Pius XI, and comes to almost dramatic fruition in our own time, in Vatican II and in the writings of John XXIII, Paul VI, and John Paul II.

A Model of Social Spirituality

By taking such a broad perspective we gain insight into what is going on today. Because in some cases, especially in America, people were not exposed to the full implications of these social teachings—except in very specialized areas of ministry—many now feel the change as sudden or condensed rather than as evolutionary. It sometimes helps to look at a paradigm. Take Thomas Merton as an example. Later I shall use his own evolution in spirituality to demonstrate a point, but now I wish to point at one element of his conversion toward a more social spirituality. The passage, which always has struck a cord in my own thought and heart, is contained in *Conjectures of a Guilty Bystander,* where Merton told a story of his own growing sense of commonality:

> In Louisville, at the corner of 4th and Walnut, in the center of the shopping district, I was suddenly overwhelmed with the realization that I loved all those people, that they were mine and I, theirs. That we could not be alien to one another even though we were total strangers. It was like waking from a dream of separateness, of furious self-isolation in a special world, the world of renunciation and supposed holiness.[2]

He went on to say that this liberation from an illusory difference was such a relief and joy to him that he "almost laughed out loud." He continued, "Thank God, thank God, that I am like

other men, that I *am* only a man among others." He then briefly
theologized that it was a joy to be human, to be a "member of a
race in which God Himself became incarnate."

In one way there is nothing new here. Any reader of a history
of spirituality could point to similar themes of incarnation, of
recognizing God's glory on human faces. But for our times, the
accent is new. Merton sees spirituality not outside his human
condition but inside.

Beyond Platonic Individualism

To be the good monk is no longer to get away from the world
in the sense of flight, but to retreat only as a way of going more
deeply into the world. It is as though the monk refrains from
listening to the ephemeral news, not in order to neglect the world
but only as a way of understanding it more deeply. We are not
speaking only of the monk, however, but of any spirituality
today.

The spiritual person's new way of inclusion in the world is to
understand the world at those depths where sin and grace touch
the human. This shift in spirituality is one that could fit every
lay person, indeed anyone who lives an active life. Different
accents, of course, will mark each one's way of living in the
church. But a new social slant runs through all states of life.
What is new is a certain sense of responsibility and involvement
in the world, and how these impinge on one's very interiority
before the Lord. This is not only a new social posture but a new
spiritual one as well. This model also capsulizes a movement
away from the Platonic individualism that has weighed so heav-
ily in spiritual thinking through the centuries.

By "Platonic" here I mean the tendency to emphasize the
spiritual in a way that undervalues the importance of the structures of this world. And by "individualism" I mean the illusion
that each one is saved, like so many individual atoms, with the
world around seen merely as a neutral stage within which one
worked out her or his salvation. Naturally it would be an utter
exaggeration to label all pre-Vatican II, or pre-Merton, or even
pre-Enlightenment spirituality as completely Platonic and individualistic. We are talking of accents here, or emphases. More-

over, there is not always evolutionary progress. It may well be that spirituality in the more organic societies of the twelfth and thirteenth centuries was far less individualistic than a person born into the industrial capitalistic world of the twentieth century could ever appreciate.

But in general it is safe to say that we are witnessing a new understanding of the social reality. And in this understanding fundamental human development becomes not merely a social concern, but has clear spiritual implications for gospel living. For many this assertion would seem too obvious to mention. Alfred North Whitehead had a phrase for this kind of obviousness. At certain times in history, he said, an idea became the "form of the forms of thought." The very idea that a spiritual life should issue in a sense of responsibility for social structures of living has become in some circles so pervasive and acceptable a thought as to be hardly adverted to as new. This does not mean that the modern age is necessarily successful in the effort to integrate the social and the spiritual but only that the hope and the vision of integration has clearly appeared on our age's horizon of thought.

Theologically one can put the idea very simply. Christian spiritual living always has recognized both horizontal and vertical dimensions. The vertical represents our worship and union with God. The horizontal is characterized by our social caring for our brothers and sisters. The insight of our day is to see how intrinsically they are related.

Jesus was never more clearly giving glory to his Father then when he lay down his life for us. The paradox lies in this: when we are most caring for our brothers and sisters (horizontal) we are pulled into a transcendent worship of God; and similarly when we are in deepest communion with God, we are pulled into communion with all humanity. This does not mean that our work for the poor excuses us from prayer. We shall deal with this later. For now it is enough to point to the profound unity between the horizontal and the vertical; thus we see the spiritual dimensions of the social. For now it is enough to cite Paul's very simple theology. "The whole law has found its fulfillment in this one saying: you shall love your neighbor as yourself" (Gal. 5:14).

1

The Structure and the Spiritual

When we talk about a new social spirituality, we are naturally implying that our relationship to God flows over into good works for our neighbor. But we have said above that the new social sensitivity goes further. It implies what we can call for want of a better name the "structural" dimension of the social. Later chapters will cover this point more fully. But it is well to introduce the idea now, since it is central to today's spiritual insights.

Theologians (such as Peter Henriot and Thomas Clark) give a helpful teaching on the meaning of the "structural" by distinguishing three levels of spiritual living: (1) the intrapersonal, (2) the interpersonal, (3) the structural. The *intrapersonal* signifies the person's unique individuality before God. This is not to be caricatured as though it implied an individualistic spirituality. Not every relationship between God and one person can be so caricatured. There is a relationship between oneself and God, between the Christian and the living Christ that is healthy and necessary. It is to be nourished by prayer and contemplation, love, thanksgiving, and praise. The literature of the ages on the stages of prayer, on active and passive dark night, on mystical gifts is to be respected.

The *interpersonal* dimension is a second aspect of social spirituality. The theology surrounding it is familiar. It says simply that love of God must overflow to love of brothers and sisters. The author of the First Letter of John gives us the classic teaching: "One who has no love for the brother he has seen cannot love the God he has not seen" (1 Jn. 4:20). This has always been a clear teaching of any spiritual school. This interpersonal dimension of spirituality helps us to see other persons as manifestations of God himself. My brother or sister becomes the epiphany of God for me. In other terms, my brother is a sacrament of God's love, my sister mediates God to me. They become a "sign" of God, a sign that contains the reality itself, the love of God himself. Think, for example, of the most basic theology of marriage. Wife and husband are sacraments to each other, symbolizing God's love for his people. This interpersonal dimension of the social has always been a basic spirituality. It has a familiar ring to nontheologians, to all Christians. It is the stuff of ordinary sermons and conferences.

But it is the category of the *structural* that is not so familiar. We have not often thought of how our spiritual life relates to social structures. What does this mean? Most clearly it means that not only does our love of God overflow to our brothers and sisters but it also impels us to regard the social structures that affect those brothers and sisters for good or evil. While the reader understands this intuitively, it may still be helpful to draw the point out more carefully.

Today, in an industrial-technological society, we are dependent on a complex meshing of patterns of distribution for our most elemental necessities. Economy, food distribution, capital loans, housing, employment, welfare, social security, education—all of these are governed by an intermingling of various social structures. On these structures depend how well we eat, sleep, think, grow old, and sometimes even how we pray. We are, in Pope John's word, very "interdependent."[1]

It is true that the bottom line in social thought is always persons. The dignity of the individual will always be a human, moral keystone. The bottom line will always be how much we love persons. In many cases we must recognize that even this interpersonal love must not only *want* the goodness for the other (*benevolentia*) but must attempt effectively to bring about good for the other (*beneficentia*). And this implies sometimes that we be present to the other at the right time with the correct help, both spiritual and material. For this to happen today, we must be dependent on many beneficial social structures. Father Chenu, the French theologian, put it well when he said that today we are not only neighbor to another, but also *socius*. He meant that our lives on this planet are tied together not only by the geographical happenstance of living close to one another. We are also *associates* (*socius*) to one another through the complex weaving of interdependent structures. It boils down to this: how I grow not only materially but even spiritually is influenced by social structures; and conversely, my own growth in spirituality has an impact on structures. Let us take a look at some serious implications of this.

Both Good and Evil Structures: Searching for the Good

The first implication is that structures do have moral values embedded in them. They can be good or evil. They are rarely neutral. Sometimes a structure is so deeply oppressive as to be unredeemable. Think, for example, of structures of social segregation in twentieth-century America. They had become clearly inhumane and oppressive. But not always are things so clear. Sometimes structures contain a mixture of good and evil. That is another way of saying that they often have elements of hurtfulness and helpfulness, elements that foster the dignity of some and may conflict with needs of others. For example, not every form of welfare bureaucracy is necessarily impersonal and demeaning. Indeed we must recognize the many humane elements of welfare distribution even when it is poorly administered.

This awareness of both good and evil delivers us from a modern mindset where one too easily sees all structure as evil, or all bureaucratic impersonalness as evil. One must sometimes look more carefully. The Manichaeans of old saw all matter as evil and thus took a dour glance at all human forms of living.

Similarly today one may want to turn back the clock in an unrealistic demand for overly simple forms of interaction that just cannot exist. Let me illustrate the point by continuing to use welfare structures as an example. The liberal may criticize the welfare system as demeaning in its manner of administration. The conservative may criticize certain provisions in welfare legislation as a disincentive for work (often, this criticism, I fear, is a mistake). But neither the liberal nor the conservative should lose sight of the great gift of God that is present when a family can

eat and have heat and clothing, precisely because history has
evolved a structure to help those who are out of work.

A knee-jerk criticism of all structures of aid to the unemployed misses a basic goodness in the history of human-
patterned ways of helping one another. This is the new
Manichaeanism. All bureaucratic ways are almost automatically
adjudged as totally evil simply because there are some deficiencies. Social structures are often like human personalities. Pieces
of our personality are evil, but in eradicating the evil we must be
careful to treasure the good that is often the flip side.

A multinational, for example, by the autonomy of its operation may be exploitive. But perhaps with just a few powerful and
balancing and regulating structures in place, some multinationals could end up becoming forces for good. Perhaps they
could be restructured to become the very force that pulls the
world away from the warlike tribalism seemingly endemic to
nation-states. A healthy spirituality relates to social structures,
then, in a discerning way. This discernment includes a theology
of sin, but also a regard for the basic goodness of God's creation.

Graced Structures

This brings us to an important insight. Structures not only
reflect God's creation, but also his redemption. (Again, I am
indebted to Thomas Clark here.) Structures that enhance human
dignity become a way of mediating God's goodness. In this sense
these structures participate in the grace of Christ, which has
entered human history. The theology need not be complex, nor is
it in any sense reductionist. Today we realize how a good
theology of redemption includes a theology of creation—and
vice versa. Creation in Catholic theology is always a graced creation. This has a tremendous implication. It means that human
goods are never *merely human*. To have material goods such as
health, good food, and clothing is, as the saying goes, to be
"blessed."

Someone blessed with the goodness of creation can say with
the Yahwist that the earth is good. And to know that the creation
is good is to know that the Creator is good. At the level of crea-

tion alone we can see how benevolent structures can take part in a circle that blesses the human and gives praise and glory to God.

At the level of redemption one begins to understand that every piece of food given to one's brother takes part in the New Creation brought about by Christ. Saint Paul teaches us that the work of Christ is restoring the harmony of a creation that has been subjected by sin and futility (cf. Rom. 8:20–22).

Suddenly, then, a very profound theology dawns on us. We see now a humanizing structure that brings food or health is a very real participation in the restoration that Christ brings to creation through salvation history.

Thomas Clark used the insightful words that humanizing structures become the new Bethel. At the risk of being prosaic, allow me to draw the image out, since it is so important.

Just as God revealed himself to humanity in Jacob's dream about a ladder descending from heaven, so a humanizing structure can also be an epiphany of God today. A man, by being able to give his children food and health care, can sense that he has encountered the God of salvation. In other words, structures that yield bread for the poor take part in and are the result of God's historical saving intervention in human history. His saving grace embedded itself in Abraham's and Moses' leadership, the kings, the prophets, and finally Jesus, and from Jesus into the church communities when they shared with the poor, took up collections, preserved education in monasteries, founded hospitals, and taught the poor.

After the Renaissance these religious communities sometimes passed the control of great, merciful structures to the "secular" world when some of these works and benefits were provided by governments and unions and hospitals, by mental-health clinics, by retirement pensions and social security. In this way, the poor man and the elderly woman, the unemployed father and the third-world farmer can eat a meal with their families and say that, in that meal, they have experienced the angel of God coming down the ladder of this new Bethel.

To speak then of beneficent social structures is to recognize a further extension of the incarnation of God in Jesus and the embeddedness of his saving work in history. In this way we are getting at a solid yet simple theology behind a new social spirituality. This is not an abstract doctrine. Rather, it means something concrete. No one need fear that structural work for the poor is simply secular or merely humanist or merely accidental to one's vocation as a religious or as a Christian lay person. After the Lord Jesus' coming, humanism, human welfare, is always a piece of the Divine.

Paul VI put this humanism in correct perspective in his encyclical *Populorum Progressio,* saying, "What must be aimed at is complete humanism. And what is that if not the fully-rounded development of the whole man and of all men?"[2] Here he is speaking of a Christian humanism. It includes a working for human well-being and an openness to a spiritual life with God.

So we have come full circle. One must integrate the interior life and social concern. But that integration is being seen today as more intrinsic and more necessary than ever. We have looked at the general outlines of what is seen as a *new* social spirituality. We have examined one dimension of just what is new in that it includes the human as agent and the human as inevitably involved in structures, and we have seen how such a concern is not merely a social concern, but genuinely spiritual.

A good summary insight would be to recall the thought of Nicolas Berdyaev. This great personalist philosopher saw that the care that one has for one's own bread may be called a secular concern, but when that person begins to care about the neighbor having enough bread, then that concern fully deserves to be called spiritual.

2

Global Awareness: A Spirituality for Worshiping in Spirit and Truth

How could an international social awareness be connected with Christian spirituality?

International awareness on the face of it seems very secular: the material of political science, economics, ideologies of every kind; whereas "spirituality" is a word used to designate our life with God, our prayer life, our interior maturation in union with Christ in the Holy Spirit. The first answer to this question is familiar and traditional; it is also an eminently sound theology. It is to say simply that real spiritual living implies a caring for those who are in any way impoverished or oppressed. Our love of God must show itself in love of neighbor. And "neighbor" today has to include the situations of sufferings in the poor countries. Let us pursue the question more deeply.

Outwardness: A Form of Transcendence

How can we understand that a concern for people on the other side of the world is something more than just a good ethical follow-through to an authentic spirituality? How can we see that a global concern is indeed a spirituality *in itself?* The meaning of this will become clear as we go on. But for now let us note merely how global awareness pushes us into some form of human outwardness. By "outwardness" I mean some movement of the individual beyond his or her isolated self. In the context of spirituality, a movement beyond the self implies something of transcendence. And any time we are speaking of a human mov-

ing beyond the self, we are beginning to touch upon the movement toward the very transcendence of God. To understand this,
let us for a moment recall a philosophy of moral action. It involves the classical question of what makes one action good and
another action not good.

Today, perhaps more clearly than yesterday, we perceive certain human actions as good not simply because of an extrinsic
ethical command but because they actually cause something to
happen within our interior life. Certain actions and attitudes are
transformative. They make us different. Seeing actions as good
simply because they were commanded was the mistake of the
nominalists of the fourteenth century. A deeper ethical tradition
saw not that something was good because commanded, but
rather, that it was commanded because it was good. Let us extend this central ethical insight into a spirituality. Think, for
example, of the command that a husband should love his wife,
and vice versa.

Sexual Outwardness as an Illustration

When a husband loves his wife, something happens within
him that is new. He moves beyond family ties, beyond peer
bonds, to the woman who is different, other, outside. His love of
his wife is not simply obedience to an ethical command flowing
from his love of God. Rather, the very *outward* movement toward his wife actually discloses something of the true God. Before this encounter with the one outside himself, his image of
God may have been deficient, and thus to some degree, the god
of his images is a false god. Now the husband's movement outward becomes a new spirituality, a new self, a deeper unity with
God. Why? What is happening in his love for his wife is that he
is pulled beyond a certain inward turning on his isolated self,
and to this degree he is being pulled beyond a kind of god of his
own concept, of his own idol-making. One can see then, in this
case, how concern and love for his wife is not merely an ethical
demand that stems extrinsically from his love of God, but an
intrinsic element of his very love of God.

From this simple example, we can jump to our question of an
international spirituality. When a man or a woman begins to

move toward a recognition of other races and other nations, he or she is being pulled outward, away from an isolated self where only a false god can be found.

Transcendence: The Movement beyond Narcissism

Charity may begin at home, but it is never allowed to end there once one has a sense of "others." To say this is more than to be clever. The point is that when we interact *only* with those *at home*, those *like us*, there is an inevitable risk of narcissism in its starkest sense. Narcissism is significant here. It is the death of a real Christian spirituality. The most fundamental point about the myth of Narcissus is that he fell in love with his own reflection and ended destroying himself in the effort to embrace that reflection.

So a charity that "stays at home" risks being simply a mask for self-centeredness. To serve only those who are like oneself is to risk serving one's mirror image reflected in those at home. And then the very god that is worshiped may not be the true God at all. To put it in gospel terms, it may be that one is *not* worshiping in spirit and truth.

This is why racism, for instance, is so deadly. It not only injures the person who is of different color, but destroys the racists themselves. For racists have built into themselves an in-group mindset, and their love for the in-group quickly becomes a caricature of love. Their spirituality becomes a bogus one. The god of their worship is in-group, inward, ultimately an idol.

We are today in a position to see that moving beyond the boundaries of one's country is not merely a sound ethical norm for the spiritual person, but can be at a fundamental level a step toward an authentic spirituality. It may be worthwhile to take the time here to unfold the thought step by step, since it is a fundamental Christian insight and so important for our times.

A Scriptural Vision: Worship of the Living God

In the Hebrew Scriptures there was no norm more basic than that which insisted that the guest be welcomed; the alien in their midst was to be treated well. It was a fundamental law of hospitality. This religious instinct of the Hebrews seems to be brought to full flowering in the early church's vision of Jesus. What could have been a more central event of the early church than Peter's recognition that the Gentiles were to be included as God's people? His vision at the home of Cornelius shocked Peter into moving beyond his own Jewishness (cf. Acts 10:17–43). Could there be anything more fundamental to the New Testament than this insight of universality, of inclusivity, of breaking down barriers between Greek and Jew, slave and free, male and female (cf. Gal. 3:27–28)?

This is a familiar teaching, but we have not adverted to its implication for our own spirituality. For the early church to move beyond a one-sided meaning of Jewish election clearly required the gift of the Spirit. Notice how this is a movement outward, and how it ends in actually disclosing to early Christians a deeper understanding of who Jesus was, of who his Father was, and of the plan of salvation. Now we are beginning to see what it means to say that a love of the outsider is not merely an ethical command of the New Testament, but a deeper vision of God, a worshiping "in spirit and truth."

We come then to a deeper theological sense of what a global spirituality might mean. To be touched by the otherness of a hungry African child, for example, is important not only because it nurtures a human life, but because it actually transforms one's own inner self and ultimately one's very vision of who Jesus is and who his Father is.

Suddenly international, or global, awareness is seen not just as a new "social justice," but as a way of assuring that the God of our worship is not an idol of our own inward consciousness. Global awareness becomes a way of assuring that the God worshiped in our churches and assemblies is the living God and not merely an icon of ourselves. So this specific form of outwardness is a helpful guarantee to make our spirituality authentically spiritual, that is, a worship that truly is "in spirit and truth."

A Christian Schizophrenia

There is a widespread schizophrenia in our world, a split between spirituality and social justice. It is not just the ordinary split between worship and living at an individual level. To some degree this will always be with us as long as humans are sinful. The split I am speaking of reaches into the very understanding of what worship is and what it implies. We have seen in recent decades many efforts—and some successes—to heal this split. More and more one reads and sees examples of interaction between spiritual living and social concerns. Articles and books are being written on integrating the two. In this chapter I wish to examine one aspect of this integrating, namely, the way in which spirituality can open us up to issues of international scope.

The very existence of the term "social justice" as it is used in religious circles indicates a problem. It almost sounds as though it were an optional specialization; as though one could have a spirituality that avoided social-justice issues.

In many church-related areas there are "Justice and Peace" committees—in colleges, religious orders, dioceses, parishes. This is a curious compartmentalization. Is it simply a legitimate need for administration and specialization in a complex church? Or is it a sign of a lack of integration? Perhaps both.

However, when committees become mere administrative buffers, when somehow peace and justice issues are never seen as "ordinary" areas for pastoral instruction, then one can begin to suspect that there is still a schizophrenia in the spiritual living of church people.

Connections between First and Third Worlds

There is a similar problem when one speaks of first world and third world. Sometimes one ends up speaking as though a social spirituality is necessary only if one lives in a radicalized missionary situation such as El Salvador or Guatemala. It is as though people in the *first* world can leave issues of social and economic liberation to Latin American theologians, or as though such concerns in the first world can be left solely to the "Peace and Justice" people of the various diocesan or religious-order structures.

This neglects one important fact, namely, that what goes on in the third world is intimately connected with what goes on in the first and second worlds.

When one makes a spiritual retreat, he or she makes it in a

center, perhaps in New York or Chicago, Ontario, or California. It is no cliché, however, to note that what the retreatant eats and drinks and wears is connected with our own economic and trade policies. The very air we breathe is related to policies that have impact on third world peoples and on our relation to them.

This is not a new thought. But somehow the schizophrenia runs deep; somehow we need to keep making connections. It is easy to forget.

Some have said that liberation theology cannot be translated into North American spirituality. Many flowers of the Southern Hemisphere may not grow in the north. They say that it may be difficult for the American middle class, for example, to perceive themselves as "oppressors" for many good reasons. But while many points of liberation theology may be unsuitable for North America, still we cannot write off certain central insights easily.

Are not some elements of liberation thought just plain gospel? Can there be a spirituality worthy of the name without some concern for our brothers and sisters who are often without food, health care, and fundamental educational opportunities? Indeed this book in numerous places points to aspects of liberation thought that are in fact mainstream Catholic social teaching for the universal church. We cannot escape fundamental Catholic Christian teachings by saying, "Well, that's liberation theology," or "That's for Latin America."

No spirituality can neglect the reality of oppression for so many of our neighbors. More than that, we cannot neglect at least an effort to penetrate some North American connections with what is happening beyond our seas.

Admittedly those connections have to be handled carefully, delicately. One has to be wary of painting with too large a brush, inducing forms of guilt that are fruitless and perhaps even un-fair. But one cannot pretend that connections between North American economic patterns and the poverty of many in the underdeveloped world do not exist.

Examples of Caring Spirituality

The first and most obvious example of how a caring person can begin to make some social connections is in the area of overseas investments by the large multinationals. To be fair, let us immediately grant that we are not engaging here in an over-simplified or automatic condemnation of multinationals. Multi-nationals can be a force for good if there is a deep sense of responsibility and some effort at careful analysis of their struc-tures. Paul VI touched on a key problem that we all must ad-dress. In 1971 he described multinationals as "new economic powers . . . which by the concentration and flexibility of their means can conduct autonomous strategies which are largely independent of the national political powers and therefore not subject to control from the point of view of the common good."[1]

This is the key. A Christian spirituality must have some sense of the common good, some sense of responsibility, some stew-ardship over economic and social realities. Profit is not evil. The questions are always, how much profit, when does it become exorbitant and end in injuring the common good?

As early as 1973 the United States Catholic Conference be-came specific by asking the United States government that it give a logical extension of the Sherman and Clayton Antitrust acts by regulating the multinationals. At that time the bishops suggested remedies that were both moderate and realistic. One remedy was to legislate some moderation of profits extracted from a third world country.

Nor was this some romantic unrealistic request. For example, if American companies in Chile had held to the rate of profit made in their other worldwide operations, perhaps the chain of events that led to the overthrow of Allende and the harsh repression of the Pinochet regime need not have hap-pened. The United States involvement in those events is a matter of congressional record. Unfortunately the widespread apathy of Christians in America is also a matter of record. At first glance such concerns sound far distant from ordinary spiritual-retreat conference material. Nor do I mean to say that every spiritual director or spiritual conference must deliver informa-tion on limits of profit ratios for multinationals.

But there is a form of naiveté, an economic and social inno-cence, that is not spiritually healthy. The existentialists call it "bad faith." When spiritual direction takes place, as it were in a social vacuum, without taking any cognizance of these matters, there is the *appearance* of neutrality. But in some cases the spirituality is not really as neutral as it seems. Let us take a case in point.

At the very time Catholic Christians were being hunted down by military and paramilitary forces in Chile after the Pinochet government gained contol, there was little in the ordinary religious climate of America to cause discomfort to business persons working with those companies who had branches in Chile. There was some help from President Carter's human rights policies. There was some religious-moral indignation in the face of overt violations of human rights, but somehow the economic and social groundwork of the Chilean repression remained unexamined. The conventional spirituality, by trying to remain above what may seem on the surface to be mere "ideology" or "politics" or "economics," in fact actually nurtures a kind of lethal oblivion.

Good people just do not seem to notice what is going on. Too many Christian businesspersons of goodwill are not moved to exercise their power by asking questions, by examining corporation and government structures that may be helping to nurture the atmosphere of repression in Chile or in many countries in Latin America—just to point to one area. Such neutrality ends in risking subtle forms of complicity with repression and violence, which will be a scandal to the history of Christianity in the West. "Good faith" has a way of becoming bad faith by its own way of "not seeing," by its own way of "having eyes that do not see and ears that do not hear."

To take another example, when Sisters Ita Ford and Maura Clarke of Maryknoll, Sister Dorothy Kazel of the Ursuline Sisters, and lay worker Jean Donovan were brutally killed in El Salvador, there were, thank God, some stirrings in North American churches. Perhaps this is the cost of our awakening: the martyrdom of women who do nothing but give humble service. But the awakening of North American Catholics must go further than outrage over overt acts of brutality fostered by repressive elements in El Salvador or other countries. Indeed some of the outrage must be purified of nationalistic elements. That is, American Christians need to be outraged not just because these women happened to be Americans, but because they represent thousands who have similarly been martyred as a result of their fundamental efforts on behalf of the poor.

Acts of violence and repression are often not merely incidental aberrations of an unfortunate dictatorship. Rather, they stem from a system of violence and repression that too often has connections with economic structures of the more affluent world.

Uncovering these connections is not easy. Sometimes they are not simple connections. One has to be wary of the temptations of finding easy scapegoats for structures of oppression that have been built up over decades, even centuries.

Let us continue more precisely by citing one economic mechanism that impinges on a social spirituality.

If one's heart can move outward to a Mexican peasant or a Brazilian peasant, one begins to unravel layers of economic connections. For example, the entire phenomenon of "cash cropping" is invariably related to Western consumption patterns and certain issues of trade. Whether it be coffee, tea, fruits, or vegetables, there has been a constant pattern of large Western companies allying themselves with elites in the third world countries. What results are third world economic systems attractive over the short run but harmful over the long run.

Again one must guard against oversimplifying. Not every operation of multinationals in the third world is necessarily evil. Much good undoubtedly has been done, and in many cases there has been goodwill and responsible efforts toward humane policies. But sometimes the very systems that have grown up over the years make humane responsible concern for people difficult. Growing a few products for export to multinationals may give needed capital to a third world country, but in the long run it can also inhibit the nurturing of independence in those countries. Even for a lay person in economics, it is easy to understand how a country that has only a few items to export is soon at the mercy of the buyer. Also, too often a level of technology suitable for the first world is imposed on the third world. Just a simple case in point: large tractors that are capital intensive rather than labor intensive can distort employment patterns in a third world country. Also, land acquisitions by the third world elite who run businesses in their own country end up being suited to first world needs rather than to basic needs of small farmers and their workers in their own country.

All of this may seem remote but it is not. It is as close to us as a business meeting of any of the top two-hundred American companies held at a local Hilton Hotel. For example, a group of conscientious Del Monte stockholders one day, because of their spiritual concern, decided to pass a "Land Acquisition Resolution." This happened in 1968. It was a surprise to many. The resolution simply asked for information on Philpak's operation. Philpak was the name of Del Monte's subsidiary in the Philippines. And these shareholders were sensing their affinity with the effect of Philpak's policies on the people of the Philippines. This is how close things are to us, a shareholders' meeting at a local hotel.

I have mentioned examples of social events in Chile and in the Philippines that have surprising connections with our own spiritual living. Hundreds of other examples could be mentioned: for instance, the efforts of the Bread for the World movement, founded by Arthur Simon, to rectify the terrible fluctuation of grain prices, so that third world countries will not be subject to forms of unfair competition.

Even closer to home is the entire structure of trade and tariffs between the developed and the developing countries. James McGinnis, in his excellent work *Bread and Justice,*[2] details how the "New International Economic Order" proposed by a large coalition of third world countries could be the centerpiece for beginning to fulfill some of the basic justice components of Christian social teachings over the years.

Unfortunately, in some United States media, the proposals of the New International Economic Order have been made to look as though they were simply forms of "reparations" demanded by third world radicals. Yet some American economists have noted how the proposals, in many cases at least in principle if not always in detail, are the only way toward fulfilling the long-range self-interests of the Western industrial countries.

McGinnis's work is still very useful and would be a fine primer for groups of Christians to begin their "outward" movement.

He provides lists of organizations already in operation and
excellent practical tips for beginning a spirituality of concern for
those beyond one's border.

Does It Fit Spiritually? Elements of a Process

What then can we do to shift our spirituality to encompass
these concerns? We cannot be unrealistic. Not everyone can
unravel economic causalities. Not everyone can integrate easily
concerns of the poor nations into a retreat or a meditation. We
cannot be artificial or contrived. We do exist where we are and
must be in some way who we are.

Yet we cannot get off the hook too easily. We must be who we
are. We in North America must also be open to spiritual change.
We cannot be artificial in our efforts to make every retreat encompass social issues. But neither can we afford the luxury of
social naiveté. Our failure to make connections may be a cause
of wonderment to later Christians who weigh us by the judgment of Lazarus. They may wonder how we could be going
through many of our spiritual retreats and homilies in ways that
neglected the ill-fed, ill-housed people right beneath our noses.
It may be that the present spirituality, which neglects these issues, deserves to be labeled "artificial."

It is not only for the sake of the poor, but for our own sake.
Because it is we who end up spiritually deprived by our lack of
consciousness. Notice how in any effort at provoking social
awareness, even in seemingly abstruse economic areas, something deeply spiritual is afoot. The process goes like this: a first
world person becomes interested in something outside his or her
ordinary day-to-day living, and begins to empathize across barriers with the plight of an individual Filipino farmer, for example. This leads one to question one's own, home-based cultural
atmosphere.

In this way, people begin to question certain things that have
been taken for granted. They begin to see some flaws in their
country, their people, their social mechanisms. (In healthy people these insights are weighed with other positive points, lest a
certain unfair nihilist attitude develop.)

People begin to search, to question, to uncover, and maybe are ostracized a little. Then new insights into their own lives surface. One can see how this simple movement outward comprises the stuff of true spiritual growth. It tends to involve people in a process that breaks down false idols of familiar living; it loosens some false attachments and even cuts away at inherited images of the self. There is a certain "un-belonging" that people experience when they begin to question the taken-for-granted social matrix in which they live. And this sense of un-belonging, or loss of "at-homeness" has something to do with the first stages of the traditional dark night of purification.

I believe that God is truly at work in the hearts of people whose social caring leads them into these spiritual deserts. Now we can begin to grasp how global awareness is indeed a spirituality.

3

Bread-breaking and a Pastoral Care of the Milieu

Ignazio Silone, in his celebrated novel *Bread and Wine,* tells the story of a communist revolutionary in prewar Italy. The character, Pietro Spina, is a hunted man, and in order to escape he assumes the identity of a priest called Don Paolo. The "priest" hides in a small mountain village of Pietrasecca and is given board in a little room above a tavern. One evening he overhears the peasants downstairs in the tavern. They are playing a card game called *settemezzo* in which the king of diamonds is the trump card. This evening there is a disturbance. It seems that the deck of cards is so worn out that the king of diamonds is recognizable from the back. So an argument breaks out as to whether or not they might substitute the three of hearts.

Some say it would be all right if they could all agree. Others say the king of diamonds is the king of diamonds and anything else would be "unnatural." Then someone suggests they call upstairs to ask the priest. Don Paolo tries to get off the hook, but they insist. So he answers. First he convinces them that players like themselves thought up the game in the first place. Then he adds, "If this card varies according to the players' whim, it seems to me you can do with it what you want." "Bravo, bravissimo," some yell. But one objects, "A king's always a king." Don Paolo responds, "A king is a king as long as he rules. A king who does not rule is an ex-king." Then he tells them a story of a far-away country where a king no longer rules. Finally he says, "So play *settemezzo* however you like and goodnight."

Settemezzo, Social Structure, and Theology

The key point of the story is, of course, that things do not have to be the way they are. *Settemezzo* is the symbol for the social, cultural, historical world. Not only the peasants in Silone's novel, but all of us have not quite understood how deeply human construction, rather than God or nature, has influenced the social reality (I use here Berger and Luckmann's term without necessarily using their ideology). Especially have we not quite grasped how deeply this social reality, once it has been formed, tends to control our processes of thought and feeling and to constrict our imagination as to what could possibly be changed in social realities.

Perhaps two quick examples will help concretize this insight that has become common today but not common enough. Take the area of food. Food has always in some way been bought and sold. It would hardly ever occur to us, given such a history as we have been given, that food perhaps ought not be the free-market commodity that it is. (I hasten to add that various controls, subsidies, and trade restrictions have made food far less free-market than the enormous agribusiness combines would have us believe.) We take for granted that the state should pay for education. That it might have a role in food catches us by surprise.

Several years ago Bread for the World, a world food lobby initiated by the imaginative Lutheran pastor Arthur Simon, almost single-handedly converted both houses of the United States Congress to the concept that everyone had a right to food. This seemingly innocuous statement may yet carry a potential for raising moral and social consciousness in this country in ways yet unmeasured and unrealized. My aim here, however, is only to point out one area where a history of social reality has tended to limit our imagination and initiative. At the very hint of a broader state role in food pricing and distribution, some would cry, "That's socialism!" The fact that education has long been seen as a human right without being considered "socialism" is an insight that does not easily penetrate the popular psyche. The game of *settemezzo* has been set up and it controls especially our slogans.

A second example would be the area of welfare. Even social

liberals tend to be obsessed lest a welfare system unwittingly reward the "lazy." Such an issue may indeed be a valid concern, but the fact that it becomes a national obsession indicates a type of blackout of other concerns that should be manifest. For instance, one finds it difficult to sustain in the popular imagination the equally valid concern over indirect subsidies "handed out" to the upper middle class and the affluent in the way of tax deductions on mortgages and capital gains—not to mention forms of corporate allowances.

Here again the dominant class has a way of setting up the popular image of the socioeconomic game of *settemezzo*. It controls our priorities, images, and emotions. As a layman to these complicated worlds I do not pass judgment on any details of welfare or tax reform, or on the merits of indirect subsidies in keeping a stable economic equilibrium. My point is more modest. It is simply to indicate how we are all pulled into playing the game uncritically. This is basically a sociological insight and one, thank God, that is beginning to penetrate the common consciousness. There are, however, theological implications of the social insight which can influence our moral, pastoral, spiritual, and even eucharistic thinking.

Church Teaching

The social encyclicals from *Rerum Novarum* onward recognized that certain structures could be constructed by humans. Vatican II gave recognition to the fact that it is not only individual humans who are to be saved, but the world itself. The *Pastoral Constitution on the Church in the Modern World* is a key document in this regard. The document sees not only individuals as sinners to be saved. It sees, rather, that "Christ was crucified and rose again . . . so that this world might be fashioned anew according to God's design and reach its fulfillment."[1]

If the world itself is to be renewed through the paschal mystery, then the pastoral apostolate of the church shares in this work of history always under and through the grace of the Lord of history. It is recognized that men and women have a new consciousness that "they themselves are the artisans and the authors of the culture of their community," and this recognition of responsibility is seen as a new "spiritual moral responsibility."[2]

The same document is direct about the moral implications of this insight: "profound and rapid changes make it particularly urgent that no one, ignoring the trend of events or drugged by laziness, content himself with a merely individualistic morality."[3] The same paragraph draws this out by speaking of our obligation to assist "public and private *institutions*." These insights have been further sharpened in the years following the Council. For example, Pope Paul's urgent word in his letter on the eightieth anniversary of *Rerum Novarum* asks us "to perceive an original application of social justice and to undertake responsibility for this collective future."[4]

One need not multiply quotations. There has been a veritable sea of official statements from encyclicals to world synods to episcopal conferences to the chapters of religious orders. The point is simple: there has been an explosion of awareness—not merely of radical theology or liberation theology but official awareness—that the church in its pastoral ministry has a responsibility not only to heal the individual players in the game of *settemezzo,* but to evaluate critically and shift the rules of the game itself.

Many parish priests and religious as well as lay leaders understand this shift and are dedicated to working it out in their own ministry. But the problem is *how.* It is easy to state grand schemes, to speak of world structures of trade and food distribution, to support the New International Economic Order for the underdeveloped nations, to recognize the madness and scandal of armaments and military budgets, but to integrate these blossoming insights and concerns into day-to-day work is a problem that frustrates many men and women of goodwill.

No easy answer is proposed. This author feels the problem all too acutely in his own work to offer any facile solutions. I would like to sharpen our reflections, however, on the problem itself. For if the problem stands out in all its starkness, sometimes our imaginations are given wider scope and provoked to new insights that may be helpful.

Moving away from Privatized Pastoral Models

What we are about here is no small thing. It requires a deep shift in our understanding of pastorship and apostolate. The key model of pastoral work has been the "one-on-one." Surprisingly, the renewal of theology did little to remedy this. Johannes Metz in his famous insight of several years ago has taught us that the existential thrust of much postwar theology, as needed as it may have been, fell unwittingly into a very private vision of human reality.

Here I would like to make the point that not only has this occurred in theology but in the world of pastoral ministry and moral education as well. Indeed I fear that what is seen in many seminaries and university clusters as liberal innovations are in reality a new fixing of pastoral models once again into the basic one-on-one. Field-education programs and clinical pastoral-education programs have developed techniques of theological reflection in which the models are predominately one-on-one. Pastoral situations are narrowed down to situations like the hospital visit, interaction with the terminally ill, or the nursing-home patient.

Even the theological "case method" becomes all too easily narrowed down to a reflection on human reality that is quite individualized. The case has the advantage of being immediate. It is now; it is "real." The person in need is at the door. Theology that speaks of pastoral "skills" all too often means therapeutic skills for handling the troubled. "Healing" has become the all-pervasive word, and no matter how much we might like to extend its meaning to the social milieu or to a social structure, its original context of one-on-one is a medium that determines the message of just what the word "pastoral" means.

Karl Rahner many years ago had some unkind words to say to any notion of the word "pastoral" that implied a basically anti-intellectual bias. My concern here is not only the anti-intellectual overtones of what goes under the name of pastoral (always a continuing problem for Americans); my deeper concern is to indicate how such a pastoral image neglects the social milieu in which the apostolate itself takes place.

An Apostolate of the Milieu Itself

Not only must we be concerned about the social milieu in which an apostolate of healing of individuals takes place. Rather, the milieu itself is an apostolate. French and German theologians immediately before and after World War II used the word *Mesology*. It is a word little heard in the English-speaking world. Its basic meaning is that pastoral concern reaches out to the *messis,* that is, to the harvest taken *in globo,* not merely to individuals in the harvest. Milieu here includes socioeconomic, cultural, and even psychological elements that are subtly entrenched in institutions.

Today a pastoral counselor knows very well that all the pastoral efforts on behalf of a troubled teenager will be washed away if the unhealthy dynamics of the family constellation are left unaddressed. The application to any form of evangelization is obvious. Individual conversions will be far too fragile if the converted heart is left in a milieu that inhibits any realistic flowering of that conversion. The human is never merely an isolated *esse.* We are both *esse ad* and *esse in.* That is, we are never healed or converted totally unless our relationships to others as well as our relation to the world and its history are healed.

These are not accidentally human. They are constitutively so. No wonder then that the words of the 1971 Bishops' Synod have been so often repeated: "action on behalf of justice and participation in the transformation of the world fully appear to us as a constitutive dimension of the preaching of the gospel. . . ." This is not only to defend action on behalf of a milieu of justice; it is to recognize that without such work, all the best-intentioned efforts for an individual will be subverted.

Healing Skills Subverted

Take, for example, the way in which existential psychology has been baptized within the last several decades. Church people found that the insights of a Maslow or a Rogers could, if handled well, be a significant and even necessary help to their pastoral work. Further, pastors have utilized group insights from Gestalt psychology as well as depth psychology and the now popular transactional analysis. Further, awareness of cognitive and affective development (Piaget, Erikson) has been applied to moral learning even in classroom settings (Kohlberg, Fowler). All of these can be great gifts to the church.

Unfortunately, all these gifts can be subverted in the blinking of an eye. We are witnessing in our time what has been termed the new narcissism. A spate of best sellers are teaching half the country how to use psychological dynamics in a way that does indeed "look out for number one." True enough, not all the literature is self-centered. There are legitimate insights into self-affirmation, self-image, self-assertiveness that can be reconciled with that sense of human integrity that is necessary for any agapeic love to be truly healthy and authentic. But there is an undoubted social tendency that is pushing the legitimate concern for integrated wholeness down the slippery slope to an individualistic narcissism.

Some would say that the seeds of such a deterioration were already present in the very structure of the various Human Potential theories and movements (Christopher Lasch, Peter Marin). I would not feel competent to make such a judgment. But it might be suggested that there is a poison in the social atmosphere that can abuse the best of theories and the best of movements in ways unforeseen by their authors. In other words it is not enough to look at a narcissistic use of a gifted psychological skill and explain it away by a simple reference to the capacity for selfishness in each individual. It is not enough to say merely that anyone can abuse a good thing.

The pastor must look more deeply. Is there something in the economic workings of a consumer society that practically forces people (against their own best intentions and goodwill) to become isolated selves over against other isolated selves? Sociologists such as Max Weber and Ferdinand Tönnies said long ago that such competitiveness (as is implied in a work such as *Your Erroneous Zones*) would be practically inevitable in the unorganic community nurtured by the new industrial capitalism (*Gesellschaft*).

This is not to say that the pastor must sponsor an all-out drive for a new socialist state. Such broad strokes of judgment on our society are too easily pretentious. Suffice it to indicate how a whole development of pastoral skills can be easily co-opted by pathologies in the social atmosphere. I am suggesting that pastoral ministers cast a critical eye before they accept totally the therapeutic emphases in ministry. If half the energy, time, and money that have been spent on developing therapeutic skills could have been put into social analysis and community renewal, the church's impact on our society and on individuals as well would be much stronger.

Perhaps an example will help. Pick up an issue of *Psychology Today.* Notice that its advertising seems oriented to the consumer interests of an upper class. I am told that among its subscribers is a high number of clergy. Now, move down the library shelf to *The Catholic Worker.* No glossy pages, a different form of advertising, and also an insignificant number of clergy on the subscription list. (I know there are elements of unfairness in this illustration, but I hope not so unfair as to be totally off the point.)

At least this much is clear. We can be experts at smoothing out the adjustment of the players of the game of *settemezzo.* Maybe they will adjust to the problem of everyone getting "one-up" on the other players by sneaking a look at the back of the cards to find the one that is crumpled up—the king of diamonds. But then maybe there is a better solution. It seems a long-run solution, but in the end its impact is perhaps sharper. It is the solution of trying to build a new community with a new set of rules for the whole game. This is a real work of the Spirit. It is a new imagination. It is to make "all things new," to do a "new thing."

The Realism of Bread and Wine

As pastors in Christian history we cannot do everything. We can only be instruments of the Lord. Unless the Lord build the house we labor in vain. We do not own the Word that builds a new community; we are only "servants of the Word." Papers have been written, and written well, on the problem of "burnout" among those in social ministry. It is apparent by now that pastoral work that addresses itself to the milieu leads to conflict, to dryness at times, to a certain lack of personal gratification, and surely to a lack of obvious and tangible success. It is a work that places us into what Thomas Merton calls the modern desert. True, no one should enter the desert imprudently. There are demons there. One must undergo a deeper conversion and one with rich affective resources.

Perhaps we could all help it to become less of a desert, less of a burn-out risk, if we could do away with the label "social ministry." That is, if we could see *all* ministry as social. Roman Catholic theology, if read rightly, proposes no sacramental ministry that is not social. There is no social ministry that is not sacramental. James Wallis warns all that they must bring to social concerns a sense of grace and hope that is our gift as Christians.[5] He speaks of how we must become the body of Christ not only as individuals but as a community of believers. He speaks of "creating communities of life, faith, and hope. . . ." We cannot talk of social issues merely as sociologists or politicians but as believers.

We end this chapter where we began. In Silone's *Bread and Wine* Don Paolo, the communist in hiding as a "priest," ends up disillusioned with the way the party is going, with the purges in Russia (Stalin's), with the dogmatism and rigidity that neglects the individual. His hero turns out to be an old priest, Dom Benedetto. He was a priest who combined a concern for the world and its social structures without ever losing the sense of human sharing, the sense of the "bread and wine" of life, the bread and wine of living interaction with individual people here and now. The cause never submerged the individual, and the individual never submerged the cause.

Christianity is bread and wine. It is bread-sharing and cup-sharing. It is the body and blood of Jesus poured out for us in a way that radically changes the rules of the game of *settemezzo,* and yet never ceases to make his loving presence felt to all the individuals playing the game. It is the bread and wine of the final kingdom-banquet made present here and now, a kingdom of justice and peace.

4

Pope John Paul II and Social Concern: *A Clarifying Note*

John Paul II's talks defy easy categorization. Clearly there is a manifest concern for conserving; but not for conserving "national securities," or so-called Catholic civilizations, or alliances between church and government hierarchs. Rather, the conserving seems to be aimed at finding a way to anchor a solid theological base for the church's work on behalf of justice. It aims at giving all liberation work its deepest Christological and ecclesiological root.

The Central Thesis

There is a central current running through Pope John Paul's talks. It is a Christological affirmation that Christ and his message transcend the political. He does not say that Christ's message has no implications for the political, but that there is always something beyond the political. In his address opening the Third General Assembly of the Latin American Bishops at Puebla, he makes this very clear:

> In some cases either Christ's divinity is passed over in silence, or some people in fact fall into forms of interpretation at variance with the church's faith. Christ is said to be merely a "prophet," one who proclaimed God's kingdom . . . but not the true Son of God, and therefore not the center and object of the very gospel message.

He continues this central point:

> The gospels clearly show that for Jesus anything that
> would alter his mission as the servant of Yahweh was a
> temptation (Lk. 4:5).[1]

The Risk of Misunderstanding

In a curious way these were risky words for John Paul to utter.
Anyone familiar with the history of Latin America knows how
reactionary forces in church and society can co-opt orthodox
words for their own ends. There are always those who will use
words such as these to evade their Christian responsibility to
analyze social situations and to act for justice. Unfortunately the
stakes are high. The words of John Paul have already been used
against priests, Brothers, Sisters, and lay people who do indeed
believe in Christ and have followed his Way even to the point of
imprisonment, torture, and death. The truth is that John Paul's
dialectic is a careful one, which tries to avoid misunderstanding.
One sometimes wonders if the constant misunderstandings are
not themselves part of the powers of darkness. The misunderstanding directed against those who struggle for justice seems
similar to the misunderstanding against Jesus himself.

The Connection between Social Liberation
and the Church's Mission

One point emerges clearly from his talks at Puebla, in Brazil,
and in the Philippines: the pope was not condemning liberation
theology's central concern that a concrete word be spoken by the
church and by church people against specific acts of repression
and injustice. Nor was he condemning any priest or bishop who
enters the public realm with a clear protest against concrete injustices. It is true that he has been concerned that priests avoid
partisan politics. Unfortunately his concern here has been misunderstood. There are those who misapply his prohibitions
against the clergy's involvement in partisan politics.

Partisan politics is one thing. The radical call of the gospel
demanding respect for the dignity of all men and women is quite

another thing. Let us be specific. John Paul II in his trip to the Philippines confronted President Marcos in dramatic fashion and said a very direct word: "Even in exceptional circumstances that may at times arise, one can never justify any violation of the fundamental dignity of the human person or of the basic rights that safeguard this dignity."[2]

We know that if ordinary priests or Sisters or lay persons made such a direct confrontation in the Philippines or in many Latin American countries, they would immediately be accused of mixing politics with the gospel. Ironically, in some places they would be told that they were violating John Paul II's admonitions against priests in politics.

Take another case in point. In speaking to sugar-cane workers on Negros Island, in the Philippines, Pope John Paul supported free associations of workers protected by law. He also repeated a theme often stated at Puebla and in Brazil that the land is a "gift of God for the benefit of all" and it is "inadmissible to use this gift in such a manner that the benefits it produces serve only a limited number of people, while the others, the vast majority, are excluded from the benefits which the land yields."[3]

Everyone knows that a lay leader giving voice to these words would be immediately called a Marxist. And in El Salvador and Guatemala and Argentina, such a person could be picked up, tortured, and killed. If these words were spoken by a priest, he would be told that he was indulging in "liberation theology," that he should not be mixing politics and the pulpit, or that he should stick to "spiritual things."

This same reaction is beginning to appear in the United States. Groups of Christians who dare to speak a word of protest against a government policy or against a multinational policy in the third world are discredited in subtle ways, if they are not outrightly labeled Marxists.

Common forms of discrediting efforts are "the Sisters are naive," or "unrealistic," or the protesters are "uncompromising activists." Sometimes one even hears that the bishops are "unwitting tools of the Marxists."

The point, then, is that the pope was not only not condemning priests or Sisters who say a concrete word in behalf of justice; he has himself been an exemplar of using the pulpit to speak to those points where economics and morality meet, where the politics of human rights and the mission of the church touch.

Nor is it correct to say that the pope condemned liberation theology as such. There has been a misunderstanding among the press and among church people on this point. People talk about liberation theologians as though such theologians were concerned only about political, economic, or social liberation. Critics even go so far as to equate liberation theologians with violence. To be clear, let us recognize that "liberation theology" encompasses a mass of material from many diverse theologians.

It is a caricature to sum it up by saying that liberation theology dilutes the gospel, or loses a sense of transcendence, or embraces violence. I do not mean here to defend all liberation theology or every theologian writing in such an accent. There may be some who need correction and amplification and balance. Most theologians do. There may be some who apply just-war teachings and the teachings of Thomas to justify the use of guns as self-protection against the violence of repressive security forces. Not all do. Some press for total nonviolence. The point is that easy labels in this complex area tend to be downright defamatory.

For example, it is a calumny to imply that all liberation theologians turn Christ into a revolutionary, or Christianity into a social program. On the contrary, as I struggle through the works of Gustavo Gutiérrez or Juan Luis Segundo and others, I am hard put to find any such stunted description of the mission of the church or of Christ.

The pope seems to recognize this. Speaking of a need for a univeral theology of liberation, he said: "The task of theology is to discover its true significance (the true significance of the liberty 'by which Christ has liberated us') in diverse and concrete historical and contemporary contexts." He then added concretely: "It is necessary to call by their names injustice, the exploitation of man by the state, of institutions, of mechanisms of economic systems and of regimes operating so often without sensitivity. . . . It is necessary to call by name every social injustice, discrimination, violence inflicted on man against his body, against his spirit, against his conscience and against his convictions."[4]

Following through on the Other Side of the Pope's Dialectic

The pope does not misunderstand his own words. In his talk at Puebla, while acknowledging that the church's mission is religious, he states that it "cannot fail to consider man in the entirety of his being."[5] Lest there be any doubt, he places himself squarely in the mainstream of recent social teaching, saying that the church's "evangelizing mission has, as an essential part, action for justice and the tasks of the advancement of man."[6]

John Paul's dialectic, if it is followed, far from pulling church people back from social concerns, will, rather, encourage them. His theology is timely, for it gives to hesitant ones or to those who travel in a dark night a secure sense that they are all about a church thing, a godly thing, a thing of God's spirit.

5

Eucharist and a Spirituality for Justice

It is one thing to have a social teaching, a theology of the social. We also need a spirituality for social application. Eucharist is a central act of spirituality in the church—not in the sense of a private devotion (it is not properly private), but as an important element of a spirituality, central to everything a Catholic knows about worship. Eucharist for Catholics and many other Christians is part of the everyday emotion of religious living.

That is why it is important to reflect on how Eucharist can lead to work for justice and how justice can lead back to Eucharist. John Paul, as we saw in Chapter 4, is carefully asserting a doctrinal basis for social struggles. He says that the church's word of healing must be a radical word—radical in the sense of its touching the very roots of evil. So the words of the church are always "both/and" rather than "either/or." It is always *both* the spiritual *and* the social; it is *both* sin *and* its systems of injustice. This total awareness is groping for a spirituality today, and a spirituality needs a worship practice, even a devotional practice, to give it life.

A spirituality is nurtured anew in the church when something becomes spontaneous. Church teaching today has done its job of making the church aware in a fresh way of the importance of the social. But this has not yet entered into our spontaneous life and feelings. We know all the statements, but the structures of the psyche and our emotions do not yet connect the social and the spiritual. Let us then consider how the Eucharist can give us a solid base for nurturing a social spirituality by choosing cer-

39

tain special needs of a social justice spirituality and seeing how eucharistic insight can cast helpful light upon these needs.

I have chosen five special needs that arise in any work for the "least of the brethren." First, the need for unity, since social concerns are complex and have a way of dividing; eucharistic models of social action can help to unite. Second, the need for self-sacrifice demanded in social justice work; eucharistic theology can teach us about sacrifice. Third, the need to understand that social work can exhaust us by its dryness and lack of easy gratification; eucharistic faith also knows about a certain darkness and dryness. Fourth, the *public* historic needs that social caring must meet, which seldom await the timetable of an easier, more private spirituality; so Eucharist is a public act yielding reflections on the doctrine of discernment of spirits, which can take us beyond individualistic and private spiritual forms. Fifth, the eschatological patience necessary in caring for the poor; Eucharist can teach us this patience, this noncontrolling, nonviolent spirit.

Eucharist and Unity:
The Splintering Tendencies of Social Concerns

Nothing can divide so easily as social issues. One notices how quickly certain social groups splinter. Social analysis is like the tower of Babel where we find ourselves speaking different languages. Eucharist, on the contrary, is an assembling of people rather than a disassembling. This is not merely a doctrinal essence of Eucharist; it is manifested psychologically and emotionally as well. Have we not experienced it ourselves as we stood around the altar—our anger or our righteousness melting a little as our eyes met the tired or fearful eyes of a colleague who had become an adversary?

People in peace groups have told me how terrible were some of their experiences within their groups toward the end of the Vietnam War. So many ideologies trying to analyze such terrible complexities. No wonder there were bitter struggles among co-workers. Paul VI admonished us to have a humility that "will rid action of all inflexibility and sectarianism."[1] In celebrating Eucharist, however, something happens—even experientially. Peo-

ple begin to realize that there is a hierarchy of truth and of levels
of existence. We begin to understand that we can disagree at one
level of existence (on a strategy, for example) but that we can
also be united at deeper levels of existence: the level of our common humanity *in the Lord*.

Eucharist can be approached in a way that takes us beyond
ideology. This does not happen magically, nor does it happen
easily. It does demand a constant purification of heart. If we are
not careful, Eucharist itself can easily be turned into an ideology. We can use Eucharist to further some ideas over others.
More subtly, we can impose an artificial unity that spiritualizes
honest differences out of existence. In doing this, we blunt the
prophetic voice for fear of creating disunity. We end up in bad
faith, subtly making Eucharist affirm the status quo. A false
"separate peace" results rather than an authentic struggle for
just solutions for justice' sake.

This need not happen. Of course, there will always be some
lack of authenticity, some context of sin until the Lord comes
again, but there is in Eucharist a dynamism that moves against
inauthenticity. The epiklesis of the first eucharistic prayer calls
down the Spirit so that we may worship "in spirit and truth."
There is in this great prayer a centuries-old intuition that no
human place or human act totally grasps God's justice. Jesus
tells the Samaritan woman that "an hour is coming when you
will worship the Father neither on this mountain nor in Jerusalem." Then he says: "Yet an hour is coming, and is already here,
when authentic worshipers will worship the Father in spirit and
truth" (Jn. 4:21, 24).

Eucharist offers now the gift of final unity, but it impels us to
struggle for that unity. "Such is the sacrifice of Christians,"
Augustine said. "We, the many, are one body in Christ."[2] When
people try to work in the complex areas of social and economic
concern, they recognize that unity is indeed a gift of God's
Spirit, and that only the Spirit can prepare them as one bread.

Thus eucharistic piety can help us fulfill one of John Paul's
concerns, namely, that the church stay church. The Eucharist
begs us to try to keep assembling. Pope John Paul said at Puebla
that the church, in its commitment to the needy, "wishes to stay
free with regard to competing systems, in order to opt only for

man."[3] In Eucharist we opt for the human at the deepest level. We opt for becoming brothers and sisters in the Lord.

Eucharist and Self-Sacrifice: The Gift of Christ's Cross

A second gift that Eucharist brings to a social spirituality is the gift of Christ's sacrificial dying. This may seem prosaic—but perhaps we need to be introduced to this central truth in a fresh way. The 1960s and 1970s saw in Catholic circles—happily so—a desperately needed recovery of the sense of Eucharist as a supper meal. Now we have matured enough in this recovery to be able to hear in a new way of the sacrificial dimensions of this meal. After all, we dare not forget that Eucharist celebrates not just any supper, but the *last supper,* the bread that the Lord took "on the night before he died." We dare not forget what the early fathers insisted on, that the Spirit sent to give us unity is the same Spirit sent from the pierced side of the Lord Jesus crucified.

The sacrifice-dimension of Eucharist is important for those who work in cities and among the poor. In our cities there is both sense-deprivation and spirit-deprivation. I will not go into all the issues of "burn-out" and all the excellent material written of late on this phenomenon.[4] It is enough to remind ourselves here that work among the poor is not romantic. There is little beauty, little gratification, little visible accomplishment. In a sense, the poor have nothing going for them, nor is there anything going for those who labor among them. It is the desert. It is the place of demons; it is also the place of miracles of grace. To resist the drift toward the more attractive life is a miracle of God's grace.

What does this have to do with Eucharist? Eucharist has a way of sharing the commonplace, the homeliness of stripped humanity. It is the one ritual act that gathers the community as it is—not the colorful, effervescent people of cocktail-party circuits—but the everyday people of a workaday world, sinful people with holes in their psyches. It is the ritual act that occurs over the most humdrum of foods: a wafer of bread and a cup of wine. God acts in the ordinariness of life, and in a eucharistic faith that can accept the ordinariness of city deserts as well.

Eucharist and Human Exhaustion:
The Dark Night in Work for Justice

There is a way in which nothing seems to change in many poor areas. City streets remain city streets. Graffiti on the wall at night are on the wall next morning. So also in Eucharist. All our lives we have been taught that the substance changes but the accidents remain. In Eucharist the Lord is not manifested in easy signs of power. He is indeed not the wonder-worker. He remains the suffering servant, the hidden one. Elements of Mark's Gospel, we are told, were redacted to confute an early spiritualism, a "God-Man" (Theos-Aner) theology. Jesus becomes a hybrid, his humanity unreal, and the cross a fiction. But Mark does not let us forget Jesus was man and that he went to the cross and died. Sinful city-structures continue to crucify people of good heart. The substance is changed by the faith, hope, and love of God's people and by God's power, but the Christian cannot forget how real are the appearances that remain. Social evil is intractable.

There does not seem to be any easy deliverance from the dark night of faith. So also in a eucharistic piety: faith must deepen to go beyond appearances. When we were children, the wine may have looked like the precious blood. As adults we are tall enough to peer into the cup and know that its contents look very much like wine. The venerable *Tantum Ergo* said it well: "Praestet fides supplementum sensuum defectui" ("Where all the senses fail, faith takes over"). The apostolate of justice moves from faith to faith, from faith that God works in the Eucharist to faith that God works in the city.

Eucharist and Public Needs:
Crucifixion and the Discernment of Spirits Purified

The eucharistic theology that speaks of a desert, of a night of faith, of a sacrificial crucifixion, will be a theology that yields a new accent in the use of the discernment of spirits. This is a different accent from much post-Vatican Council II fare. Slogans sometimes reflect the signs of the times. The slogan that said we are an Easter people and Alleluia is our song (referred to by

Pope John Paul in New York's Harlem) may have symbolized a
needed emphasis for the time. But when people who work in
justice issues take a look around, a good look around, I suspect
they are more inclined to sing that we are a Good Friday people
and that our song is more aptly a Kyrie. Kyrie on battered
spirits; Kyrie on rundown houses; Kyrie on tired, discouraged,
and uncertain apostles.

In the discernment of spirits a certain sense of harmony can be
seen as a criterion of the presence of the Spirit. Ignatius himself
was not simplistic here, and good spiritual directors have known
that this discernment can be a tricky business. The key caution
here is that the peace which is the sign of the Spirit is not the
world's peace. It is not necessarily that psychological sense of
well-being central to the narcissistic society. Especially in areas
of justice, there are obligations that do not fit harmoniously, nor
feel peaceful. New obligations sometimes require a new person,
a new *me*. And a new *me* requires the death of the old *me*. There
can be peace here, but often no more visible to the naked eye
than is the body and blood of Christ in the Eucharist.

Even the timing in discernment is different. A spirituality for
doing justice requires that we do justice in its time, not our time.
It is like dying. We must die when it is time to die. And Eucharist
by its very nature can give us a good sense for this. For by its
very nature Eucharist is social, not just individual. One goes to
mass when it's time for mass. This is a different timetable from
some models of spiritual direction. In a spirituality of justice, it
will sometimes be less a question of "meeting the person where
he's at," and more a question of meeting history where it's at.
Jesus' death was his hour, but it was a time out of due time, the
hour of the "triumph of darkness" (Lk. 22:53). The sign of the
Spirit is peace, but also an agony in a garden. "Father, if it is
your will, take this cup from me; yet not my will but yours be
done" (Lk. 22:42).

Eucharist and Eschatological Patience:
Concern and Justice for the Poor

In both Eucharist and justice there is a certain nonfulfillment.
Christ is present but he has not yet come in fullness. The com-

munity is present, but it, too, is still "not community." This brings a temptation in both Eucharist and justice. It is the temptation of the zealot, of the apocalyptic. It is the temptation of forcing the times. One is tempted to violence to manipulate structures or people. In Eucharist in every age of the church, the temptation manifests itself in disdain for impoverished ritual. One finds the public assembly of sinners too human for faith. It is boring because God does not appear. One would rather go to inner lights and consolations. It is a temptation of faith.

In the world of justice one demands the kingdom *now.* The 1960s found Mamma Cass singing, "There's a new world coming, and it's just around the bend." How disappointing to find that it was not around the bend. Jesus said, "The exact time it is not yours to know" (Acts 1:7). Some form of class struggle and revolution may be ethical, but the Christian cannot be uncritical. There is surely a form of struggle that is not of God. Pedro Arrupe, in an article that appreciates some aspects of Karl Marx, gives us fair warning on other aspects. He says:

> For the Christian, the death and resurrection of Christ, and not a revolution . . . is at the center of history. . . . By reason of his hope, which he places in a Christ worthy of hope, the Christian will keep a sense of realism in the face of human accomplishment. He will not disparage any effort at social progress. But he will not see in any accomplishment of this sort the fulfillment of his destiny. Apart from Christ, the men and women around him are simply human, no individual and no group is saviour—except Christ![5]

In Eucharist Christ is present not in glory but as a pledge of glory. In all things we must discern the times, the in-between times. It will keep us from becoming zealots, who bring hatred rather than love. At Puebla, John Paul said, "Jesus opens his message of conversion to everyone without excluding the very publicans." He adds what this means for the social apostolate: "There is no doubt . . . that all this is very demanding for the attitude of the Christian who wishes truly to serve his least brethren, the poor, the needy, those on the margin of society, in a word, all those who in their lives reflect the sorrowing face of the Lord."[6]

Jesus does not exclude the poor or the publicans. He eats and drinks with them. The Christian shares Eucharist with the poor and even with the publicans. One resists the movement to class hatred.

In Conclusion

Pope John Paul II carved out a model for the social apostolate of the church by holding up the uniqueness of Jesus and his mission. In this way he gave us a careful *doctrinal* underpinning for a social spirituality. A eucharistic piety can be a good vehicle for moving this *doctrine* into a *spirituality* for social justice. The Eucharist brings the gift of unity in a work where unity is always threatened. The renewal of the sacrificial dimension of Eucharist can be especially helpful since the work for the poor takes place in a desert and in a dark night. Both Eucharist and social justice demand more discernment, away from individual dangers and easy psychologisms that would falsify Ignatius. Eucharist gives a feel for the imperfection of the in-between time. There is an urgency about justice, but it is a Christian urgency. It leaves time for celebrating the Supper Meal. But those who work for the poor and for justice know that this Supper Meal is, of all things, a Sacrificial Meal that took place "on the night before he suffered."

6

Ministry in the Church and Structural Concern for Justice

In any consideration of the church and social justice one must start by citing both the clear problem and the challenge. The problem surely is that we have not been as outstanding as we should have been. Barbara Ward, in a booklet written for the Vatican Commission on Justice and Peace, speaks of guests who are invited to a banquet but have other things to do. She then touches upon the key problem for Christians in developed societies, namely, the problem of not being exposed in any concrete way to massive poverty and of therefore not developing a prophetic voice. She says:

> In this general climate of indifference, the Christian does not yet stand out as prophet or catalyst. All too many of us are simply relatively fortunate citizens who . . . are not exposed to the massive, growing miseries at the base of the world society. We are proving, if proof were needed, that it is very difficult for wealthy societies, like families or individuals, to get through the eye of the needle.[1]

Barbara Ward as an economist devoted to human life has given an example of single-mindedness. Throughout her writings she remains hopeful. She knows well the challenge, yet she sees no reason why the Christian community cannot be a worldwide "catalyst of energy, devotion and reform." She articulates the challenge in a way that sets the focus of this chapter.

> . . . if, then, with courage and persistence and the energy
> of true hope, Christian citizens are ready in season and out
> of season, to lobby legislators, rally voters, instruct fellow
> citizens, worry the indifferent, encourage the active and
> create a new kind of justice and world responsibility in the
> Church and in the nations, the world may be saved from
> the evident wrath to come.[2]

Notice that she asks for a new kind of justice and world responsibility in the church. Thus she speaks not merely of giving food
to a hungry man, but of "lobbying legislators" and "rallying
voters." If we take a look at official church teachings over a long
range, we can see in this past one hundred years a broad and
obvious evolution. Perhaps such an evolution could be understood by pointing to one man's autobiography as a metaphor.

This journey of the church is aptly symbolized by Thomas
Merton's monastic journey. A thesis by Sister Elena Maltis
makes this point more systematically. She cites Merton in his
early work, *Waters of Siloe.*

> It [monastic life] takes a man above the terrors and sor-
> rows of modern life as well as above its passing satisfac-
> tions. It elevates life to a superhuman level to the peace of
> the spiritual stratosphere where the storms of human exist-
> ence become a distant echo and do not disturb the center of
> the soul—no matter how much they may rage in the senses
> and the feelings.[3]

Then she cites the later Merton who, in his work *Faith and
Violence,* writes with different images of the monastic life:

> My own peculiar task in my Church and in my world has
> been that of the solitary explorer who [instead of jumping
> on all the latest bandwagons at once] is bound to search the
> existential depths of faith in its silences, its ambiguities,
> and in those certainties which lie deeper than the bottom of
> anxiety. It is a kind of submarine life in which faith some-
> times mysteriously takes on the aspect of doubt when, in

fact, one has to doubt and reject conventional and super-
stitious surrogates that have taken the place of faith . . . .[4]

Notice how Merton no longer conceives of himself as above and
beyond the world. He is not in a stratosphere above the terrors
and sorrows of modern life, but now at the bottom of things
where the phrase "submarine life" becomes a dominant image.
His spirituality of the 1940s does not cease, but in the 1960s it is
a spirituality that takes integrally within itself the role of social
criticism. He sums up who we are in the church today when he
says:

> That I should have been born in 1915, that I should be the
> contemporary of Auschwitz, Hiroshima, Viet Nam and the
> Watts riots, are things about which I was not first con-
> sulted. Yet they are also events in which, whether I like it or
> not, I am deeply and personally involved.[5]

What is central here is not only that a man's spiritual journey
should lead him to the welfare of fellow humans (indeed this is
true of all the saints), but that now such a spiritual journey leads
also to a *structural* concern for others. Merton is implicated in
the *world's* movement. He is, and we are, and the church is not
only helping others socially in the world as a static theater, but
taking responsibility for the very movement of the world itself,
for the very milieu of humankind.

Such an awareness is now flowering in the church and we
ought not to miss it or take it for granted. Perhaps a concrete
example will help us see more clearly. In 1830 a French pastor of
goodwill may have courageously preached to factory owners
that they must give their workers a living wage. But what he
could little understand was what Peter Berger and Thomas
Luckman called the "social construction of reality." In other
words, reality had been constructed by humans themselves in
such a way that if a converted factory owner did pay a living
wage, he would go out of business because of the competition.
What was needed was—as we know today—a new construction
of reality, namely, some empowerment of the worker through

unionization. Notice that such a new reality had to be created not only to allow workers to achieve just wages, but also to allow an employer to pay a just wage while remaining competitive.

Such an element of structural justice was recognized by Leo XIII when he said in *Rerum Novarum* that even though someone made an agreement, such an agreement (contract) could be invalid because of the unequal bargaining positions. In Leo's teaching we see the beginnings of an awareness in the church of the meaning of a *structural* reality in morality. Justice is denied not only by the individually greedy person, but through the inheritance of circumstances embedded in social systems.

The Application to Ministry

In the twentieth century such an insight has developed richly in church teaching. John XXIII in *Mater et Magistra* and Paul VI in *Populorum Progressio* applied the teachings to inequalities inherent in relations with the third world. There have even been some high points of pastoral application in the church. For example, it remains the glory of the American Catholic church that it (unlike some European sister-churches) did by and large keep faith with the immigrant workers in its midst.

Yet while the insight is old enough to trace back before Leo, it nevertheless remains a new insight in need of fresh application in many areas of social concern. Most of all it calls for fresh application in the church's ministry. Ministry must concern itself not only over individual conversion, not only over healing hearts, but also over healing structures. Otherwise the healed heart will be unable to inscribe its fruit of justice on the world itself. In Reinhold Niebuhr's classic terms, "moral man" will remain powerless and ineffectual in an "immoral society."

The word "structure" is not always easy to understand. It has many meanings in many contexts. A helpful articulation of a meaning sufficient for our purposes here is one given in the statement of the Appalachian Catholic Bishops. They speak of how the forces of corporate giants become perverted and destructive growth patterns develop. The principle of "maximization of profit" becomes an idolatrous power. Then they give a clear understanding of what an evil structure does: "This power overwhelms the good intentions of noble people. It forces them to compete brutally with one another. It pushes people into 'conspicuous consumption' and planned obsolescence. It delivers up control to a tiny minority whose values then shape our social structures."[6] They go on to point out how difficult it is for good individuals to change things when structures militate against change: "We know that there are many sincere business people, zealous reporters, truthful teachers, honest law enforcement officers, dedicated public officials, hard working lawyers and legislators, who try to do a good job. But we know too that, the way things are set up, it's hard for good people to do a good job."[7]

Such an insight by the bishops into structural evil corresponds to contemporary insights into scriptural understandings of the "powers of evil." The simple words," . . . the way things are set up, it's hard for good people to do a good job," is a perfect way to describe what theologians today mean by "the *situation* of sin." So the power of evil becomes autonomous and embeds itself into structures. These structures entrap us. They tend not to draw good from us but to draw out our worst—sometimes despite goodwill to the contrary. We have what some see here as one perspective on the original-sin tradition in the church. Obviously, then, the work of redemption, in which Jesus has given his body the church a certain share, must include a healing of this history of sin. Thus the very baptismal function of induction into a saving community implies a ministerial work to heal structures.

The Domain of Gospel Ministry and Arthur Simon's Parable

The foregoing ushers into focus a problem, namely, how can work for structures remain a gospel work and not merely become a social-secular work? Arthur Simon, the founder and leader of *Bread for the World,* tells a parable that helps us understand this problem of placing work for structures into ministry. Once there was a farming town that could be reached by a narrow road with a bad curve in it. There were frequent accidents on the road, especially at the curve, and the preacher would preach to the people of the town to make sure they were

Good Samaritans. And so they were, as they would pick the people up on the road, for this was a religious work. One day someone suggested they buy an ambulance to get the accident victims to the town hospital more quickly. The preacher preached and the people gave, for this was a religious work. Then one day a councilman suggested that the town authorize building a wider road and taking out the dangerous curve. Now it happened that the mayor had a farm market right at the curve on the road and he was quite against taking out the curve. Someone asked the preacher to say a word to the mayor and the congregation next Sunday about it. But the preacher and most of the people figured they had better stay out of politics; so next Sunday the preacher preached on the Good Samaritan gospel and encouraged the people to continue their fine work of picking up the accident victims.

The parable recall's what Paul Ricoeur says about the human person's new awareness, namely, an awareness of being in relationship with others in structured ways, that is, not merely as "neighbor" but as *socius.* Father Chenu, a French Dominican, calls it the new way of charity. He says that man has always been social, but he adds: "Today, not accidentally but structurally the collective event lends scope and intensity to the social dimension—human love treads these lasting paths, these organizations of distributive justice, and these administrative systems."[8]

The problem, then, is very real. When is ministry for life religious and gospel, and when does it become secular? What work for life is natural and what is supernatural? What is gospel and what is humanism? The questions are age-old. And without presuming that the church today has completely solved the problem, I do think a good part of the answer is already within the church's official grasp and official teaching.

In official meetings and synods, papal and episcopal teachings have addressed the problem and have given us enough of a theological answer to go on. Let us cite chosen, illustrative texts from the Catholic context. First, Vatican II's *Pastoral Constitution on the Church in the Modern World* has many comments on the subject. But one celebrated section is as follows: "While we are warned that it profits a man nothing if he gain the whole world and lose himself, the expectation of a new earth must not

weaken but rather stimulate our concern for cultivating this one.
. . . Earthly progress must be carefully distinguished from the
growth of Christ's kingdom. Nevertheless, to the extent that the
former can contribute to the better ordering of human society, it
is of vital concern to the kingdom of God."[9]

The World Synod of Bishops of 1971 and of 1974 each dealt
with the problem. We have already seen how the 1971 Synod
called work for justice a constitutive dimension of preaching the
gospel. In 1974 Pope Paul, after citing the danger of losing the
religious dimension of our mission, said this: "There is no opposition or separation, therefore, but a complementary relationship between evangelization and human progress. While distinct
and subordinate one to the other, each calls for the other by
reason of their convergence towards the same end: the salvation
of man."[10] In the human rights document of the 1974 Synod, the
bishops used a theology of the divine image and taught that the
"integral development of persons" makes clearer in man the
divine image. Then they said: "Hence, she [the church] believes
firmly that the promotion of human rights is required by the
gospel and is central to her ministry."[11]

Summarizing this brief set of quotations, we can say that healing the structures of irreverence for life and of injustice is part of
the ministry of the church, because such healing is "of vital concern to the kingdom of God" (*Gaudium et Spes*), "a constitutive
dimension of preaching the Gospel" (Synod 1971), "required by
the gospel and central to the Church's ministry" (Synod 1974).

Why take time to cite these examples of official documentation? First, awareness that such insights are now mainstream
official teachings will keep us from being intimidated by those
who would accuse us of humanism or of becoming social agencies. But more than that: it is to underscore that the concern for
structural justice and the concern to place the struggle for structural justice within the mission of the church is not merely a
concern of a Daniel Berrigan, of a Helder Camara, or of a Latin
American theologian, but rather, it is official and central teaching within the Catholic church.

Most of all it is a matter of rejoicing not only that such an
insight is found in official teaching, but that it is making its way
into the popular religious psyche of our people. At the 1976

Eucharistic Congress in Philadelphia, when people struggled to
touch Mother Theresa, they were struggling to touch, in this
case, not someone known for mystic gifts such as Padre Pio, but
someone known for simply picking people up off the streets of
Calcutta. But more than that, the people also welcomed Dom
Helder Camara. And those who knew his history, knew that his
life has been a different struggle from that of Mother Theresa.
Dom Helder symbolizes not just an enormous interpersonal love
for the weak, but also the struggle for justice against systems of
dependence and exploitation.

Dom Helder in the midst of his talk at the Philadelphia Civic
Center walked over and embraced Mother Theresa. I like to
think this embrace was more than a kinship of courageous people. Rather, I see a symbol of two forms of ministries-in-the-
church meeting and embracing. And in a way, Dom Helder's
emphasis is a struggle that poses the most important challenge to
church leaders. His work is less clear, more risky, more apt to
provoke misunderstanding even among his own people, and yet
all the more urgent today.

The Problem of Ambiguity

Yet this ministry that attempts to heal structures has a special
problem connected with it. I would term it "the problem of ambiguity." Many church leaders can agree that gospel includes
work for human life and human rights—even structural work.
But they rightly fear choosing certain concrete options that com-
mit the church to one economic or political view that may not be
the only valid Christian view. The point of Paul Ramsey's work
Who Speaks for the Church? was to purify us of easy assumptions that the charism of leadership will lead us to right decisions
in the complex area of socioeconomic and political affairs. This
is a common caution, perhaps, needed today. But I would like to
accent another side to the issue, which sometimes goes unac-
cented. Namely, what appears to be neutral ground is not always
neutral. Sometimes when the church refrains from taking sides
in an issue, for fear of partisanship, it has taken a side by not
taking a side. Another way of saying it is simply that sometimes
our silence speaks loudly. This may not be an everyday occur-

rence, but it does happen that situations become radicalized to the point where there just is not ample neutral ground for a large institution.

Historical examples may be clearer here. In the Germany of the 1930s was there a political neutral ground? Can we not, at least in hindsight, recognize that what looked like neutral ground was not neutral? There was a personal heroism of many priests, ministers, and bishops, yet in the episcopal statements of the German hierarchy (in the words of Gordon Zahn) there was "not even a hint of any question, of whether or not the Hitler war effort met the conditions set for a 'just war.' "[12]

Another example. In the bombings of Hamburg of July–August 1943, the dead numbered 30,000. The raids on Dresden of February 1945 killed some 135,000. On March 9 and 10 the raids over a four-mile residential district of Tokyo are estimated to have killed 84,000. On August 6 and 9 the bombings of Hiroshima and Nagasaki killed an estimated 68,000 and 38,000 respectively. The killing of noncombatants was even at that time clearly recognized as evil, yet one can find no significant *corporate* criticism of these actions. Moreover, despite Pius XII's pleas to statesmen for a negotiated peace, no official Catholic spokespersons gave sustained protest against the Allied policy of unconditional surrender—an omission that John Courtney Murray called a "classic example" of a failure to apply moral principles.

A third example concerns racism and segregation in America. It could be summed up in a symbol. The symbol is contained in the words of Leander Perez, political boss of Plaquemines parish in New Orleans. He was, you may remember, the man excommunicated for his opposition to the integration of the parochial schools (a courageous act of Archbishop Rummel). But Perez's comment was, "How come we could have slaves, separate schools and churches for these Negroes for ages and ages and now all of a sudden it's a sin?"[13]

The point in all of these questions is not historical Monday-morning quarterbacking. Indeed even at the time of these incidents there were clear teachings already in the mainstream of Catholic thought—teachings that were not applied. The point is that the church took stances that at the time may have seemed to be those of moderation or may have seemed to be prudent neutral ground. But now we know they were not. Rather, they appeared to have been examples of an immigrant church so anxious to be established that it became absorbed in the *Zeitgeist* of the times, and so lost its prophetic voice.

We may be right in our anxiety that the church not be pulled into partisan blocs, and we may be right in our anxiety not to provoke undue division in the church by too quickly identifying one social option as *the* gospel option. But we must be careful not to allow this anxiety to bring us to a silence that is an unwitting speaking in behalf of the status quo.

There is a corollary to this problem. It concerns the matter of competence. Oftentimes it is stated that a churchperson or the church cannot speak on an issue because it is complex and specialized. Surely we must be careful of easy and abrupt position-taking in the complex areas of socioeconomics and international politics.

But the deeper question must always be asked. Namely, why is it that at times we choose certain areas in which to be competent, to research carefully, and to locate personnel and resources, and other areas in which we are not? We must always ask ourselves what might be our cultural and theological biases that predispose us to give certain questions a priority. Too many good Germans said they could not protest because, after all, they really did not know enough.

Dualisms That Lead to Neglect

Sometimes an idea about ministry can lead a person of goodwill to neglect a certain gospel reverence for life. For example, I am sure that the chaplains of institutions in which recent press releases have exposed cruel treatment would be persons of goodwill. But if they observed some of the same things newspaper reporters saw, and if they did not complain in any effective way, we must ask, How did they conceive their ministry? What kind of dualisms between soul and body, between spiritual and physical, between creation and redemption must have been going on in their understanding of ministry? Has speaking in behalf of ill-treated mental patients, ill-treated children, ill-treated elderly in profit-making nursing homes, ill-treated prisoners, ill-treated homicide suspects become only a secular activity of good investigative reporting? Has the church's role in these issues of human rights totally been taken over by the secular press? Why is it that the church does not give its own equivalent of Pulitzer Prizes to those who speak well in behalf of innocent victims?

The Problem of Banality

There is a special difficulty in the effort to combat structures of injustice. We are accustomed to struggling against individual immorality where the evil is often quite clear. But the modern devil of structures is less clear. The late Jewish political scientist Hannah Arendt uttered a famous teaching. She took note of how, historically, people can easily be seduced by what she called the "banality of evil." Her prime example, of course, was Nazi Germany, and she illustrated how many good people were gradually pulled into accepting things little by little. Evil becomes interwoven with everyday structures and we tend to accept it, and to "adjust." To turn Shaw around, "We accept things as they are and find it difficult to dream things that are not."

The evil is so subtle that no issue becomes *the* issue that can rally forces for good. Everyone says, "I'm not sure this is the issue," or "It's too complex." Moreover, structural evil does not lend itself to easy scapegoating. Corporations may make decisions that will put many people out of work, but each person in the corporation seems like a very nice individual. The F.B.I. may have broken into homes and kept files on outstanding American citizens, but individually, of course, they are all very nice fellows. We forget that people get trapped in evil structures. And sometimes we are dissuaded from protesting, or our attention is diverted from the evil because we are so accustomed to connecting evil with obviously malicious people.

Perhaps this is the genius of a Martin Luther King and a Dorothy Day. Martin Luther King kept telling his people that they could not hate the white person, that the white people themselves were trapped in structures. But for all of that it did not dissuade King from pointing out the evil.

Because structural evil has a way of becoming pervasive, sometimes the people most alert to it tend either to seem neurotic or to be neurotic. Rollo May has made famous a popular insight, namely, that neurotics feel things that are wrong in the atmosphere long before the supposedly sane. They, like artists, have sensitive antennae. So when a person starts calling attention to structural evil in a consistent way, he usually finds himself being called neurotic, or we ourselves say things such as, "She's got personal problems," or "Look, he doesn't do his own work in the parish." The person may be neurotic, may not do his "own work," but this does not resolve the issue. Thomas Merton in his *Conjectures of a Guilty Bystander* reflects that whoever pushes the button for the bomb will be one who is considered emotionally a very stable person. He will have passed all his psychological tests for entrance into the security community.

When Jesus went into the marketplace to fight the *systemic* evil, there must have been those who said, "This man from Galilee seems to be a little compulsive about some of his ideas."

Matthew's Simple Theology

We in the church sometimes grapple with, and look for terms about, things that the gospel puts quite simply. Jesus left us little doubt that ministry for human life and for justice was a ministry that constitutes entrance into his kingdom:

> The king will say to those on his right: "Come. You have my Father's blessing! Inherit the kingdom prepared for you from the creation of the world. For I was hungry and you gave me food. I was thirsty and you gave me drink. I was a stranger and you welcomed me, naked and you clothed me. I was ill and you comforted me, in prison and you came to visit me." Then the just will ask him: "Lord, when did we see you hungry and feed you or see you thirsty and give you drink? When did we welcome you away from home or clothe you in your nakedness? When did we visit you when you were ill or in prison?" The king will answer them: "I assure you, as often as you did it for one of my least brothers, you did it for me" [Matt. 25:34–40].

So the church must give food and drink, visit the sick and those in prison. But food, drink, clothing, prisons, and various forms of helplessness have been institutionalized into systems and structures. We are gifted with some social power and most of all with the power of the gospel word. We are, in Thomas Merton's words, "implicated." The modern translation of Matthew's words may be something like this. I was hungry and you rallied people to back reserve grain legislation. I was in prison being beaten and you called for an investigation. I was ill-housed and you set up a group to analyze the local situation and to make suggestions, or you provoked your parishes to make critical advocacy pleas for my people.[14] I picked mushrooms and you offered support for United Farm Workers' efforts in the east as well as the west. As long as you worked for the least of my brethren against the structure of domination that oppresses them, you did it for Me.

7

Why Do Social Teachings Have Little Impact?
A Reflection

For at least the last decade—one could go back further—the American Catholic bishops have issued an extraordinarily rich corpus of social teaching, as responsible and progressive as that of any group in the country. Yet bishops complain of a *hearing* problem when it comes to certain social teachings. People often do not know what the bishops have said.

The bishops' pastoral on the moral life issued in the fall of 1976 is a case in point. So much time in the writing, such a wide and careful consultation, a relatively fine style of writing, some rather good publicity efforts, systemized efforts in some dioceses to bring the pastoral to the grassroots, and yet for all this the pastoral seemed to have evaporated into the air.

Social Content of Recent Pastoral Letters

To be fair to the bishops, if there were no church, if there were no hierarchy, if these were just a group of men assembled to consider some issues of right living and right thinking for our times, we would be obliged to recognize in their social teachings of the past decade not only a word of social wisdom, but even a word of courage and compassion. We may quarrel with this or that teaching, with this or that omission, but the large picture in social teaching could be summed up in a simple listing of its impressive insights. In the past few years this group of men has

1. spoken unequivocally about the evil of continuing racism and discrimination especially against blacks, Hispanics, and Indians.

60

2. spoken compassionately of the "human tragedies" behind the statistics of joblessness.
3. spoken in behalf of farm workers in what has become a special link of friendship—bishops and farm workers.
4. spoken of how a real-estate industry can bring about subtle but effective discrimination in housing.
5. called attention to a form of crime that sometimes goes unnoticed—white-collar crime.
6. spoken of how a penal system is "sometimes a cause of increased crime" and of how prisons are often "settings for gross violations of prisoners' rights."
7. recognized that we who live in a powerful nation must use our power for the weak and powerless.
8. applied the concept of a responsible use of power to the issue of "policies and patterns of consumption and production" in the light of their impact "on other nations and peoples."
9. have spoken not of the easier words "aid and charity" but of the more demanding word "justice" in "trade treaties, commodity prices, corporate practices and monetary agreements."
10. spoken with force of the rights of the unborn and yet compassionately of the individual woman who needs our help.

These are general teachings but they are also wise. It is tragic if bias or familiarity allows us to miss them or take them for granted simply because such truths came with a mitre. Unfortunately the episcopal writings do not seem to have impact. People, priests, religious, and bishops go about things as usual. The social wisdom has not penetrated to the everyday psyche of the church in a way that would make it an administrative priority or a spontaneous pastoral impulse.

One exception is the issue of abortion, which does have a social dimension. Since it is a social teaching that has had some impact, it is worth reflecting on for a moment as a paradigm.

A Matter for Social Involvement in the Political Arena

The unborn become, socially speaking, a category of persons and for the Catholic conscience a clear issue of human rights. When our compatriots accuse us of imposing our moral convictions on this issue, there is seemingly an unbridgeable gap of understanding. They do not grasp the depth of our conviction that the fetus is human and that this conviction implies a social and legislative struggle similar to that against racism. For the Catholic conscience it is not mere rhetoric that would see the present bias against the unborn as a new racism. For just as the face of a black man, a Japanese, an Indian has looked different enough to be reckoned less than human, so also the fetus. Abortion becomes for the Catholic conscience a clear matter for social involvement in the political arena. Here is one issue of social liberation that has taken hold of the Catholic everyday mind.

In this struggle against abortion, then, one finds the church using its social authority. Organizations for research and investigation are formed, action groups—even direct action—are given official support, local hospitals and legislators are targeted, and education programs are begun and carried through. In short, the teaching does indeed have an impact. (Nothing said here is meant to demean this effort. It seems to this writer to be a movement that is in the long run progressive, humane, theologically true, and pastorally necessary.)

The Degree of Disestablishment

There is an aspect to this movement, however, that deserves mention. Namely, the American Catholic community, which through a century of upward social movement has become well established, has in this issue suddenly become once again a disestablished minority. And to the degree to which Catholics push the logic of this conviction into the public realm, they shall be a troubling minority. An Associated Press wirephoto of Cardinals Manning, Cody, Medeiros, and Krol standing before a congressional committee to testify on a projected anti-abortion amendment bespeaks a different church-society posture from, say, the photos of John F. Kennedy and Cardinal Cushing together or Franklin D. Roosevelt and Cardinal Spellman.

Examples of Weak Follow-through

If we take a look at other areas of social teaching, we find that their logic and their application at the parish and diocesan level are pressed less vigorously. Some examples will illustrate the point.

The bishops' pastoral of 1976 speaks of unemployment and its implications. In an earlier teaching the bishops were even more specific: "We call on local parishes, dioceses, Catholic institutions and organizations to undertake education and action programs on issues of economic justice."[1] Where is the effective follow-through to such a call?

On housing, the words of the pastoral are similarly pointed, and also hark back to an earlier statement in which the bishops were explicit about what is needed at the grassroots:

It is not enough to point to the reality of poor housing and recommend that government and other institutions take appropriate action. We must also reflect on our own responsibilities and opportunities for action. We call on individual Catholics, dioceses and parishes, as well as other Catholic organizations, to join us in a new commitment to those who suffer from poor housing.[2]

The bishops then speak explicitly about the role of parishes:

With its roots deep in the community, the parish can play a critical advocacy role regarding the housing problems of its people. . . . Parish programs of rehabilitation and housing maintenance could be initiated. In addition parishes can join with others to utilize government programs and monitor public and private efforts to alleviate poor housing.[3]

Few parishes—people or priests—know of the existence of such statements. Such education and action programs haven't the structure to make even a beginning. Moreover, if there were any serious follow-through to such teachings, we would find ourselves becoming not only more disestablished from our culture, but having to face the likely problem of division from within.

We could go down the line of similar episcopal statements (to say nothing of papal teachings) asking for urgent action on prisons, peace, amnesty, race. One wonders, for example, what has happened to the urgent recommendations of *Populorum Progressio* about teaching and acting for development; or the extraordinarily fine insights into deteriorating cities and the recommendations for action contained in Pope Paul's letter to Cardinal Roy, *The Coming Eightieth*. The urgency of these appeals has a way of dissipating into thin air. Whatever follow-through they may have had, they never raised any pastoral steam.

It has been frequently noted, but deserves repetition, that the greatest concern about following the Magisterium and loyalty to the Holy Father usually arises in the context of *Humanae Vitae*, especially in connection with sterilization and other sexual teachings. The rest may be given lip service but somehow one finds very little spontaneous pressure exerted from diocesan chanceries on social issues. A priest may be called to task for violating liturgical rubrics but one will travel through many dioceses before finding a priest called to task for not applying the teachings on prisons, or for not setting up an advocacy committee for better housing.

Bishops Ought Not Be Scapegoats

Bishops cannot become easy scapegoats. We must face ourselves. In the abortion issue our people are already prepared to hear the word. Long tradition and clear lines allow it to be a whole-church issue. This readiness to hear, however, seems not to exist in other social areas. For that lack of readiness we all bear some responsibility.

How do we prepare a ready atmosphere for the prophetically taught word to find a home in us? This is a question especially for educated Catholics. Is their progressive social thinking a factor only of clever learning or is it the source of compassionate living? Are their insights into the social neglects of the church—a criticism needed in season and out of season—born of a loving solidarity with the poor? Are they pastoral groanings uttered in empathy? Or are they only intellectual realizations devoid of life-witness and commitment?

The Necessity for "Structures of Plausibility"

We must attempt to understand why some social teachings evaporate into thin air. Peter Berger's "structures of plausibility" may give us some help. In *Rumor of Angels* he applied it to the difficulty of sustaining one's faith in an atmosphere where faith is not supported. Similarly it is difficult for a bishop or for anyone to sustain a social insight or to carry an insight through to effective practical implementation if there are not structures of plausibility in the social milieu.

Neither a bishop nor anyone else can be expected to push a social teaching where the very atmosphere gives one a sense of its implausibility. When social perceptions are given no support, when a teaching disappears into a vacuum, then very soon the perception itself is lost. And certainly the capacity for "staying power," the capacity for sustaining the issue as a serious concern is gradually eroded. So, as an administrator, the bishop himself is influenced by the atmosphere. He develops an instinct for what the traffic can and cannot bear. Not consciously but surely as a presentiment he must begin to suspect who among his priests, people, religious, and university people will be around tomorrow and the day after.

Teaching Stemming from the Total Life of the Church

How does one acquire staying power unless one's life is involved in some more than academic way with the issue? In fact it is time we recognized that *sustained* concern for the poor is miraculous. One could even see it as a charismatic gift in the church. Seeing it in such perspective takes it far beyond any merely intellectual capacity for critical social analysis. And seeing it as a gift, we can groan for it individually and corporately. To be sure, we must work at it. There can be no quietistic waiting.

This is the crux of our analysis. The wirephoto of the four cardinals referred to earlier symbolized a certain new form of disestablishment. But in the wirephoto the cardinals were not dressed in the shabby attire of immigrants. They were clearly well groomed, well housed, and generally reflected the economic status of today's Catholic.

This is not to criticize the cardinals but simply to characterize the fact that economically and socially the church is largely established. And this fact of establishment surely has something to do with the lack of effective follow-through on certain social teachings. How do we follow through on social teachings and ask others to follow through when we are little touched by those issues in an everyday way? Is this a key to why the teachings issue from and tend to remain with administrative staffs or program specialists? The words of Barbara Ward again come to mind: "All too many of us are simply relatively fortunate citizens who . . . are not exposed to the massive, growing miseries at the base of the world society. We are proving, if proof were needed, that it is very difficult for wealthy societies, like families or individuals, to get through the eye of the needle."[4]

It is hard for established churches to get through the eye of the needle.

8

Social Justice and Abortion

Abortion in the United States has been generally examined through the prism of a private-morality mindset. The social questions surrounding abortion often take their starting point from an individual case. The effect is that the social dimension of the issue is immediately distorted. To clarify this point, the analogy of war can be helpful. Someone who is dedicated to the eradication of war through nonviolence is often asked if he or she would defend a little sister against a deranged rapist. The very question distorts. In an age of modern weaponry the paradigm of defending a little sister is falsifying. It misses the social meaning of modern war and the social implication of nonviolence. There comes a point in social-ethics when the accumulation of numbers is no longer a simple multiplication of homogeneous cases, but a qualitatively different moral phenomenon.

Dr. Bernard Nathanson is an example of one whose shift in thinking illustrates the movement from individual to social analysis in abortion ethics. Dr. Nathanson was a crusader for the liberalization of abortion laws in New York State. He himself ran a clinic for abortion. In the process of preparing an article on the success of his clinic, he came to a change of mind. Among other things, the sheer numbers struck him. He said: "I began to feel we had regressed from a daring, courageous institution . . . into an enormous business mill."[1] When we speak of abortion today we must use as a model not only individual cases but the "business mill" itself, namely, the total social phenomenon.

Responsibility as a Model of Social Thought

H. Richard Niebuhr, in his masterly work *The Responsible Self,* speaks of responsibility as a contemporary model of ethical activity. He contrasts this with the teleological model, in which the vision of man is that of maker, and in which the primary ethical question is: What is the purpose of this action? He also contrasts responsibility with a legal model that views man primarily as citizen, where the key question is: What is the law? Niebuhr argues for a vision of man who is first of all an *answerer,* and his vision is that of man-in-dialogue.[2] In this model the question is not what is the purpose or what is the law, but rather: What is happening to humankind and what is a fitting response? It is, I believe, a model of ethics more suitable for handling the reading of a global social phenomenon and more likely to provide a more adequate response.

It is this line of thinking that I ask to be undertaken by all segments of the community including the religious and legal communities in abortion discussion. It is not enough to ask whether a woman should bear a particular child. Rather, we must ask what is happening. What signs of the times seem to be predominant in these developing structures and institutions? Beyond what one woman's purpose might be, beyond what a law (or norm) might call for in an individual case, the deeper questions have to be: What is going on when so many children of the womb are being killed? What is going on when legal protection is no longer effectively offered even to viable children? This question is not only for faith people--Protestant, Catholic, Jewish, Hindu, Muslim, Buddhist—who for centuries have believed the child of the womb to be sacred. It is also for secularists, for it was the secular humanist wisdom that pushed into modern consciousness within this past century its own scientific realization of the humanity of the fetus. No one who is responsible can neglect this structural question: What is happening to the social fabric of a civilized protection of life and what is the response for humans who are the reponders?

Americans and Individualism

The first answer to what is happening is this: pregnancy has become an entirely private affair. Strangely, it is a first in the history of cultural anthropology. Why has this become so quickly acceptable in America? As we suggested in an earlier chapter, one answer can be found in that same individualistic ethos that has ruled many of the social structures of America and has even penetrated the religious psyche. The same individualist cultural tendencies that rationalized slavery by such words as "a man's home is his castle" can also claim that a woman's body (pregnant with child) is still an entirely private possession of the woman. Such an individualist conception of property rights calls to mind the rights asserted by the robber barons of the nineteenth century. And now, despite a half-century of progress in antitrust and labor legislation, the ethos of private property has suddenly achieved a new mischief.

The Women's Movement against Itself

The same nemesis of individualism haunts the women's movement. For the same property ethos that for centuries allowed women to be considered almost as property owned by their husbands subtly flies beneath the radar of otherwise sensitive women. It has settled into the women's movement, wounding it at its most vulnerable point, the vulnerability contained in the understandable desire for a greater freedom of decision. Yet here in the abortion issue, the formerly oppressed become the new oppressors. The dominant male ideology of "freedom to use" has done its ultimate demonic work. It has been transferred to a whole class of women who now gain their freedom at the expense of others, in this case, the children of their wombs.

Controlling Ideas and the Dominant Class

Juan Luis Segundo, in *The Liberation of Theology*, clearly spells out Marx's idea of "suspicion." It is the suspicion of how the economic system influences the ideas of the culture. One need not be a Marxist to recognize, for example, how a technology-dependent economy works its mind. In Jacques Ellul's phrase, we have become a "civilization of means." No human activity escapes the "technical imperative." In this most human of all situations, pregnancy, we *technically* "solve the problem," while the doctor uses technical language such as "terminating the pregnancy." What is most striking is the way in which the reigning "praxis" (the workings of the total system) gradually draws so many to accept the formerly unacceptable.

This insight into the power of a culturally dominant idea should not be a new insight to Americans. We of all people have realized too well how it could be that liberals, the churches, and even intellectuals were drawn into an unjust temporizing in the issues of race and slavery. Not too long ago many liberal leaders uncritically and patriotically accepted Dresden, Hamburg, and Hiroshima. I do not here accuse abortion advocates of being warmongers or racists. My analogy suggests only the way good minds are seduced by cultural biases.

Vietnam is an example par excellence in which dominant ideas seduced "the best and the brightest." Of all places, here was one where individualistic casuistry applied to social situations worked its absurdity: we ended up bombing a town in order "to save it." Each escalation had its own individual persuasiveness. But the total, terrible reality of the highest noncombatant casualty ratio in recorded history took more than six years to begin to sink into even the liberal psyche of this country. Similarly, abortion for rape or for the life and health of the mother, while it may be an inviting individualist technical strategy, becomes in its social extension corrosive of the very values it had technically hoped to pursue. One can understand why Gandhi could have been so passionately concerned for using the correct means to achieve social ends. "As the means, so the end," he said, and one could hardly doubt that he would see abortion as absolutely antithetical to that ahimsa (nonviolence) so necessary in pursuing social goals.

Society's tendency to find technological solutions causes a blindness to certain human values. Sometimes the way to heal this blindness is to show pictures of what is happening. Pro-life people show aborted children in waste-cans. Some say this is emotional propaganda, but is it not truly what is happening? Of one and one-quarter million abortions a year, surely there are many fetuses whose limbs are differentiated and who must be put somewhere. Many people were similarly upset when pacifists showed pictures of Vietnamese children burned by napalm. "Bleeding-heart propaganda," they said. But B-52 pilots began to feel the truth. Pictures helped deliver them from the blindness of a push-button technological cleanness. Pictures have a way of healing the language blindness of technological phrases such as "protective-reaction strike" and "pregnancy-termination" procedures.

In all these allusions I do not intend to categorize those who disagree with my legal, moral, or political views on abortion as militarists or insensitive technologists. But there can be no doubt that I am asking them to reconsider, to question their seeing power, to drop what I believe are cultural scales from their eyes. I ask them to look at what is happening with new eyes.

The Difficulty of Sustaining an Insight

The best and the brightest cried foul at the June 1977 Supreme Court decision allowing states to deny Medicaid funding for abortion. Many claimed that this was a class discrimination against the poor, who will not be able to have an abortion as easily as the affluent. My concern here is that even those who strongly believe in the humanity of the fetus end up absorbing the ideology of the dominant *Zeitgeist* in America. They do not sustain their insight into the fetus as human. They listen to oft-repeated ideas about the rights of the woman and, for a moment, they forget the rights of the fetus.

Perhaps the analogy of racial segregation will help people to see what is meant here. It is as though one were to say: If the rich can live in segregated neighborhoods, then let us be sure to fund the poor man who also wishes to be segregated. Otherwise, his segregationist effort may turn to violence. So in abortion funding, we hear of concern about discrimination against poor women, neglecting, of course, the enormity of the global discrimination against the fetus. Hannah Arendt's insight into how evil becomes gradually and structurally entrenched is applicable. Evil is so much with us that it becomes banal enough to be acceptable. Abortion and its technological trappings slowly crawl into the social fabric of law and institution and cultural mindset. What was previously unacceptable becomes acceptable almost through the inertia of opposing forces. Americans look back on the nineteenth-century Dred Scott decision of the Supreme Court and they are struck with wonder at the absurdity and inhumanity of such a decision. Yet, in its Roe *v.* Wade decision in 1973, the Court decided (against all legal, social, and religious tradition, against a clear tradition of tort and property law) that the child in the womb was "not a person in the whole sense," and "not yet capable of meaningful life." If there is some resentment that this decision should be labeled a new Dred Scott decision, the argument should at least be met squarely and not dismissed as rhetoric. It seems to me that such a comparison would be incorrect for only one reason, and that would be if the fetus were not human. Yet many who believe deeply that the fetus is human seem to accept, at least implicitly through their inertia, the Court's decision.

Those who do not accept the prevailing pro-abortion mentality are often made to seem as though they were merely a sectarian band of zealots. But the concept of abortion as a social institution and its conceptual comparison with race should provide some ecumenical understanding as to what the pro-life movement is all about and how it perceives itself. It sees itself not in any way as imposing a denominational minority doctrine on a pluralist society, but as a progressive force laboring in continuity with the best of the liberal tradition in the history of this country's drive for civil and human rights. Even those who disagree with this vision should, according to all rules of ecumenical courtesy, give due recognition to their opponents' self-perception.

On Not Losing One's Nerve

Some who are anti-abortion do have a way of losing their nerve or of never getting up their nerve. They fear to struggle against the Supreme Court's ruling. They begin to accept a mechanistic sociology that is merely a crass form of headcounting about how many people may or may not vote for an amendment. This form of sociology neglects the veritable blitz of the major media by which the heads became convinced in the first place. Within eight years, the media and the courts have made abortion a plausible structure. And must we lose our own will, our own sense for creating anew? Recall Rosa Parks sitting down in the front of the bus, refusing to move to the back. She did not count heads to see if the atmosphere was ready for new civil-rights legislation. There is a time and there are gifts for being wise as serpents, for being politically astute. But some must be bold enough to create the new atmosphere that changes even wise people's sense of what is politically astute. True, one must respect the ideas of another in a pluralist society. But that does not mean that one may not work to change those ideas by every politically honest means available. Racial sentiment in America was never seen as a static given; neither should abortion sentiment be seen that way. As inhumane racism cried out for enlightenment, so does inhumane racism toward the race of children of the womb cry out.

Academicisms *v.* Commitment

Yes, it is true that everyone should be pro-life on all issues. One can grant that the church has not surpassed itself in its structural implementation in behalf of other life issues. But to constantly frame this objection easily becomes an academicism in the face of the clear structural, legal, and social evil of abortion. That is, one acts as an academic spectator analyzing the church's failure in other issues. But, again, the question must be: What is happening here and what is your response?

It is also true that everyone should work at the societal causes of abortion, such as poverty, sexism, and unemployment. But this has its own way of becoming an academic analysis. Sometimes one must deal with the structural embodiment of evil even if it is not the root evil. Indeed, the social embodiment becomes a root of other worse evils if it is not dealt with. Moreover, dealing always with everything has its own way of dealing effectively with nothing. But this above all should be clear: any sociologist would agree that the rise in abortions can largely be traced to the law itself. The legal structure is the most effective teacher, and right now it is seducing millions of women a year into believing that it is perfectly fine to kill the children of their wombs.

Often one reads that the abortion debate is carried out in too strident a tone. Usually, as one continues the article, the "balanced" position proposed somehow ends up asking pro-life people to cease being "divisive" and to allow people to make up their own minds. But such advice was silent while the Court was making up everyone's mind. If one takes the humanity of the fetus with any kind of seriousness, these cries for moderation and balance call to mind similar language of Latin American landowners when they beg their striking farm workers for less divisiveness. It is a subtle academicism. It really asks for a form of moderation that is, in fact, content with the status quo. Academics may wish for a sane "bias for life" in individual decision-making, but such a wish is a straw in the wind of a sociolegal *voluntas,* which in fact has willed the death of over five million children since 1973.

There is a cultural elite in America that casts pro-life people as a conservative fringe group. But it is the dominant abortion mind that is conservative. It is conservative in the social sense of a consumer capitalism that sees a fetus as a product owned and disposed of as private individuals see fit. Some look at the pro-life movement and allow an old fear of Catholic power to cloud their judgment. Some look at it and see it as too religious. Some regret the backwardness of some of its members on issues such as war or capital punishment. These kinds of purism are a luxury the times do not afford us. In social concerns, one makes coalition with bedfellows not of one's choosing.

Someday the truth will be known, and I hope it will not be too late. The truth—which answers the question "What is happening?"—is that a great social evil is abroad. The truth, as I see it, is that the pro-life social response constitutes a progressive, liberal vanguard for a humane and civilized culture.

9

The Arms Race and the American Parish

Francis X. Meehan and William Mattia

What can be said about the nuclear arms race and the church that has not already been said? We shall not try to say something new. We write from the perspective of a parish priest [William Mattia] and a seminary theologian [Francis X. Meehan], and we are trying to catch the symbolism of that perspective. When a parish priest and a seminary theologian begin to take seriously the urgency of the armaments crisis, it is a kind of announcement that a shift in the church has occurred. It is a way of proclaiming that the time is ripe for the application of teachings that are both old and new. It symbolizes the hope that now the mainstream of the church is ready to take a new view of American militarism.

Commitment and the Professional Teacher

Whenever I [Francis X. Meehan] reflect as a moral theologian on the issue of disarmament, I sense a crisis of conscience. First of all, I am concerned that my teaching has fallen into the perennial Christian trap of individualism. One easily concentrates on individual sexual or medical-moral issues to the neglect of the social milieu that nurtures the dilemmas they pose. Catholic theologians are more mindful of a certain imbalance in their traditional approach, their preoccupation with sexual issues, for example, to the neglect of racism and militarism. But what theologians do with this recognition is the acute problem that gnaws at my conscience.

75

The issue goes deeper than discovering the proper balance in the amount of time given to social issues in my teaching. It cuts to the very meaning of being a professional theologian. What does being a professional teacher really mean? I am not speaking of the need to be scientific. Rather, I am speaking of a system in which one can teach many things but end up living none of them passionately. I cover many curriculum areas, including the topics of peace and disarmament. But the problem is this: the disarmament issue, an issue that pertains to our human survival, literally screams at us in its vital urgency. Yet somehow it ends neatly compartmentalized into a business-as-usual course. This allows it to become integrated into a business-as-usual life.

This issue is personal, but it is more than personal. It concerns others. Bishops, universities, parish schools, and, most of all, the parish priest, share the problem. It was a parish priest who provoked this reflection. He said out of the blue: "I feel I must begin to do something about nuclear arms; when are you going to start doing something?" Then he spoke about his parish: "I do not know how to handle my sense of urgency there; I do not know how to share what I feel."

Can anyone sense the urgency? And if we can, would we know how to handle it? Do I as a moral theologian treat nuclear armaments as just another topic for classroom discussion? Do bishops cover it as merely one more topic within committee discussions? Do Catholic universities feel the crisis, or is it just for the Peace and Justice Committee in campus ministry? Is the whole church just a professional teacher, socially informed maybe, but still just a teacher? The point is that in a social issue such as this, the very way we place the issue affects the substance of the teaching. It is easy to play the academician, the one who judges but never quite arrives at that special brand of efficacious judgment that involves commitment.

Were I possessed of a life commitment to peace, I think I would end up with a sharper and more substantive teaching on the issue of disarmament. This is not just an insight derived from Latin American liberation theology. In fact, it is old-fashioned moral theology. For Thomas Aquinas defined prudence as a wise choosing that is dependent on the long-range commitment of the heart in charity. Saint Augustine said: "It is only through charity that one enters into the truth." In other words, I shall not be able to judge the moral truth that disarmament teaching imposes on my life unless, in some way, I am already involved in walking toward that truth. Moral truth is not attained by teachers who climb mountains of books only to view the issues as a mere spectator. The moral truth of the need for disarmament is reached only by those who walk in the valleys— even if they must read while they walk. In the matter of peace and disarmament today, I suspect that the gospel truth is not so much a teacher's truth as a doer's truth.

The Parish Priest and the Hidden Impact of Armaments

As a parish priest, how do I [William Mattia] face the nuclear arms topic personally and as a spiritual leader? Personally, it has bothered me for some time that the church wasn't doing much (at least as far as I thought) and it frustrated me even further that I wasn't doing anything. I had a sense of powerlessness in the face of this issue. I felt I existed in an atmosphere of indifference. It was at this point that I confronted a seminary theologian about what the church has said on disarmament and what he individually was thinking and doing about it. He surprised me when he spoke of what the church had already taught. He challenged me as to what we might do together.

As a parish priest, I am naturally concerned about the ordinary everyday events in the lives of the people I serve. I am concerned about this woman's son who is on drugs; about this high school girl's social problem; about instructing this family in the faith; about preparing this couple for marriage; about consoling a family on the death of their father. Yet, surely my responsibility does not end with addressing the individual lives of my parishioners. Do not world realities, such as disarmament, also touch my people? Can I really serve my people if I do not touch upon the world in which they live?

The Parish and the Milieu of Un-Peace

I begin to realize how much my people are affected by more than just what happens in our neighborhood. I see that the milieu of the entire country has a tremendous effect on my people's consciences, on their thinking, actions, and lives. I am convinced that America's stance on nuclear armaments has a harmful and evil effect on the people I serve. Suddenly my interest in nuclear arms appears to me no longer an avocation separate and apart from my parish role. I begin to see the intimate connection between my interest in peace and my work at the grassroots level of parish living.

More and more I realize that my parishioners are filled with American ideals and dreams. They look upon themselves as Americans who are a peaceful and honest people. We have been defenders of freedom and of people in need. It becomes clear that I need not uproot this feeling among my people. Instead, I can use it. I note that even a civil religion has a prophetic pull that I cannot neglect. Now I look for ways to show how the arms race is actually leading them away from the American dream of freedom and security. I appeal not only on doctrinaire grounds; I seek to show how the arms race is not even working, that the balance of terror, while it has a certain logic, does not live up to its logic, for it is making them less secure and less free. Perhaps then I can begin to show how it is even less Christian, that what is unchristian is also inhuman and that what does not deliver in human terms is also unchristian.

I realize more and more how important are the economics of the armaments issue. The arms race is hitting the man and woman in the street where it hurts most, in the pocketbook. It would be a blessing to be able to offer concrete facts to show how it is destroying their very economy. I think they might understand how government spending ($135 billion annually on defense, 30 percent of the national budget) is increasing inflation. They could see how capital used for arms buildup is nonproductive and, in the long run, causes unemployment. Most of all, they could see that, as defense spending increases, the budget is cut for the elderly, the young, and the poor. The parish I am in has many elderly and unemployed. And so, the arms race is no longer an abstraction. In their day-to-day living, my people are harmed both physically and mentally by the arms race.

More than that, the arms race has harmed my people psychologically and morally. Our neighborhoods are tense because of racial hatreds and the mutual mistrust among people of different religions and social classes. As a parish priest, I must try to reconcile people. I preach on the need to settle differences by peaceful means. Yet there exists a certain irony in the fact that nations seem absorbed by the need to settle their differences by threats of war and destruction. There is a subconscious legitimation of violence at work, and the work of peace at the parish level is subtly undermined as the psychology of the macrocosm influences the microcosm of the parish.

Catholic Teaching and Its Nonapplication

So both of us, parish priest and theology teacher, experience a sense of urgency. Historically we have taught the just-war doctrine. Our purpose here is not to criticize this approach, nor to analyze how its application today might itself lead to a certain form of practical pacifism. Rather, we would suggest that certain clear points of the traditional doctrine are simply not applied. Saint Augustine taught that only a man who loved his enemy might kill him. "No one indeed is fit to inflict punishment," he said, "save the one who has first overcome hate in his heart." If this is Augustine's concept of just war, have we ever really preached the correct doctrine?

The principle of immunity for noncombatants and the prohibition against direct killing were certainly taught by the church long before 1940. Yet, as we saw in a previous chapter, in the saturation bombings of Dresden (135,000 killed, by conservative estimate) and of Tokyo (84,000 killed), we did not raise our voices in protest. The estimates of the dead in Hiroshima and Nagasaki are put at 68,000 and 38,000 respectively. How many Catholics, even leaders, boldly condemned this? Even today many seem prepared to accept the fact that the destruction "shortened the war," thus implicitly accepting a form of terrorist blackmail.

Nonapplication Today

We seem to have the same problem today. Vatican II taught that "any act of war aimed indiscriminately at the destruction of entire cities or of extensive areas along with their population is a crime against God and man himself . . . [and] merits unequivocal and unhesitating condemnation."[1] How unequivocally and unhesitatingly do we mean this condemnation, when nothing is ever said directly against the buildup of weaponry that has no other purpose than the destruction of entire cities? Are we quibbling over the casuistry that attempts to distinguish actual destruction from deterrence? If so, then what of the teaching that says: "The arms race is an utterly treacherous trap for humanity and one which ensnares the poor to an intolerable degree"?

The Pro-Life Model as a Way of Application

How can we find our way out of what seems a maze of insincerity? What can impel the church and ourselves to cease being ineffectual spectators who teach nonefficacious truths about peace and to become genuine witnesses to peace? Is the church only a teacher or is it also a communion of life? Is it only a teacher of ethical truths or is it a "way"? Is it only a romantic vision or is it something within our grasp?

The struggle of the church against abortion, as we demonstrated earlier, provides a clear model for our thinking. The church has found a way of enfleshing its teaching on this issue. Its pro-life stance has become a way of life. The struggle against abortion has taken place at concrete levels. We organize; we bring suit; we designate specific clinics and hospitals for censure; we ask pointed questions of candidates; we preach; we protest. We even develop careful doctrines defining when material cooperation is unacceptable. This is what is called enfleshing a doctrine. The church here is more than a teacher. The very words "Roman Catholic" have come to signify anti-abortion, pro-life. Some shrink from this, fearing that we may be acting narrowly or sectlike. But the issue is worth it. The church in this area has come to give witness to the meaning of life, creation, redemption, and love.

Following through on Our Armaments Teaching

Some may feel that armaments may be a more ambiguous issue than abortion. Yet there seems to be no ambiguity in the Holy See's statement of 1976. It said that the arms race "is to be condemned unreservedly." It goes on to add that it is a "form of theft," a "criminal act of aggression" because "even when they are not used, by their high cost they starve the poor to death." This is clear teaching. But it will remain ineffective unless we begin to live it as a church. It is a teaching that will take flesh only when we proceed as we have in the abortion issue, when we organize, bring lawsuits, designate specific companies associated with the armaments industry for censure, when we protest, when we praise conscientious objectors rather than only tolerate them, when we begin to be concrete about forms of illicit material cooperation. The teaching will become a witness when we support the equivalent of a Hyde amendment in the armaments area, when we begin to direct taxes and contributions in anti-armament directions. The teaching will become flesh when our schools become known as peace schools, just as our hospitals are known to be places where no one gets an abortion. If a public nurse comes into our school to speak on teenage pregnancy, she would be monitored, since we know how sensitive the issue is. It is time for a similar form of monitoring for military recruiters in our schools.

The Degrees of Enfleshment

All of us have different charisms. Not all can enflesh the teaching in the same way, nor will feel so called. As a parish priest and a seminary teacher, we feel neither strong nor righteous; nor do we wish to be seen as prophets. We merely suggest that there are humdrum, everyday tasks to be done in this area. They are tasks not just for the strong, but for those who sense the need for the support of a large church and even for the nurturing of its powerful and influential structures. It is time that the teaching on disarmament take its place in the mainstream of church activity.

We believe that this is not merely a social struggle. Rather, it is a struggle for the American church to maintain the very transcendence of its mission. It may turn out to be the only way the church can resist being absorbed into the secular culture of American militarism. In this sense it is not merely an ethical issue, and it may be related intrinsically to the meaning of our worship and sacraments. Resisting armaments and all that they signify today can be a way of purifying our very Eucharists so that they may truly become a worship in spirit and truth.

For some, the serious application of our teaching would mean being disfranchised in certain social and subtle ways. It has already led some to prison and to being misunderstood even by their friends, family, and colleagues. We suspect that there is certain confrontation in this issue with the real powers of evil in this world, that in touching the war economy we may be touching upon some of the same demonic systems that have visited persecution and death upon many of our brothers and sisters in Latin America.

The image of Saint Thomas More again comes to mind. We are all called to be the king's good servants, but God's first. We hope that the day will not come when we must choose between God and nation. But the greatest tragedy would be that the day would come and go without our noticing it, that the day would slip by because unwittingly and implicitly we would have signed a new oath of supremacy to the idol of national security.

As parish priest and teacher, we do not pretend or demand courageous prophecy. We only hope that we all can speak as simply as the child spoke who saw that the king really had no clothes. One does not have to be an expert to denounce the multiplying megatonnage of thousands of bombs for what it is—absurd and evil. At the parish level, it is not a matter of presenting a great theoretical analysis, not even a matter of pursuing a great cause. It becomes a matter of loving a particular people close up, enough to have their fearful eyes meet ours with a plea that we teach the word and become the word we teach.

10

The Catholic Conscience
Faces the Military Draft

What do you think of the draft? The question gathers momentum. What are the moral dimensions of the draft? There is hope too that this question will also gather momentum. In 1980 the administrative board of the American Catholic bishops gave their statement, and there is a sense of appreciation that they handled the question with some timeliness.[1] Not all the moral questions connected with the draft are simple ones. For example, there is the issue of voluntary services that, because of social reasons, may not be so voluntary. In other words, at a time of some 30 to 40 percent unemployment among young urban minorities the volunteer army may not be "volunteer."

But amid the complexity the bishops did make one very clear point. They approved conscientious objection as a legitimate Catholic option that could be "derived from the Gospel and Catholic teaching." Further, they supported selective conscientious objection from a moral point of view and asked for a dialogue concerning possible legal provisions. In other words, they gave official Catholic legitimation both to pacifists and to those who believe that a particular war is unjust. They also gave legitimation to those who choose to go to war.

The Theory Is Old, the Psyche Is New

The bishops did not speak anything new here. What may be new is its explicitness and its pastoral proclamation. There is need for a conversion of heart here, indeed a conversion of

83

mind, of psyche too. The bishops in effect ask each in his or her conscience to examine if the cause is just, and to participate only if it is indeed just. In other words, draft counseling becomes a clear moral and pastoral mission of the church—no longer to be left to our Quaker friends or to be shunted aside as if it were a radical activity of leftists. If participation in war or war prepara- tion is seen as a decision of moral conscience—and clearly the bishops see it that way—then the conversion of psyche must overflow into structures of moral guidance provided and pre- pared for at diocesan and parish levels.

The Catholic tradition of just war allows one to go to war only if the cause is just and if the rights vindicated are in some pro- portion to the evil of suffering. These have been key elements at least since the thirteenth century. For Augustine the prima facie obligation was, of course, not to kill. One could kill only in self- defense and even then only "mournfully." Unfortunately, for most of the church's history and even in recent history, we have acted as though the prima facie obligation was to go to war, and at times with very little moral mourning.

A New Burden of Proof and Discernment

Similarly in the area of pastoral counseling of conscientious objectors there has been a curious twist of moral presumptions. The burden of proof has always been shifted onto the one who would choose not to kill rather than the one who would choose to kill. The pastoral counselor scrutinizes the young conscien- tious objector (C.O.) in order to assure that his motives are pure and that he is not acting from cowardice or selfishness or lazi- ness. But the pastoral counselor rarely feels an obligation to scrutinize in any similar way the motives of those who go to war. That is, have they sufficiently justified participation in killing or possible killing by applying careful just-war reasoning? Or are they going to war simply because it is the easy way out, the way of less gospel foolishness, a succumbing to the mass mind? One expects such a twist of priorities from the nation-state and its draft boards. One should not expect it from the church of Jesus Christ crucified and his ministers. It was a pastoral mode that ended up deviating from our own traditions.

It may be understandable that an American Catholic church, after years of being kept outside and held down as unwelcome immigrants, could have fallen into an anxious nationalism. After all, we had to prove we could be good Americans and that we really belonged. What better way than to brag about how many Catholics were in the armed services, and dying for their country?

Is There a Guiding Leader?

The American bishops' statement seems to wish to make allowance for both the C.O. and the one who would go to war. They give words that lend legitimacy to both; and both here and in the past they have emphasized the importance of personal conscience in this area. They refrain in this statement from making any concrete moral judgment regarding precisely how they feel toward the actual situation today. In other words, they make no judgment as to whether war today is in fact just, or whether concretely war preparation today would involve participation in justice or injustice.

This does not imply, however, that the young person is left without any official Catholic guidance in the matter-of-fact issues. Pius XII as early as 1953 gave some concrete guidance when he said: "Defending oneself against any kind of injustice, however, is not sufficient reason to resort to war. When the losses that it brings are not comparable to those of the 'injustice tolerated,' one may have the obligation of 'submitting to the injustice.' This is particularly applicable to the A.B.C. war (atomic, biological, chemical)."[2]

The bishops at Vatican II give us guidance in that there are forms of "total war" that are unacceptable even from a minimal standard. They teach clearly that "any act of war aimed indiscriminately at the destruction of entire cities or of extensive areas along with their populations is a crime against God and man himself. It merits unequivocal and unhesitating condemnation." It seems clear then that there is an official church position that is not merely neutral toward modern war as it exists concretely. In other words, in the real world there is no longer merely war in the abstract. John XXIII gave the church a clear sense of this when he said: "In this age of ours which prides itself on atomic power, it is irrational to believe that war is still an apt means of vindicating violated rights."[3]

War's Dynamism: Beyond Individualist Analogy

The Catholic church in its recent official teaching recognizes that today's weaponry no longer fulfills the rationality at the heart of the just-war teaching, namely, the issue of proportion. The church senses that the frequent analogy thrust at the C.O. asking if he would defend his sister from a deranged rapist is an inept image. One may indeed defend his sister; but such an individualistic model has nothing to do with the social dimension of war today and its attendant uncontrolled spiral of violence and suffering.

The words of the fathers of Vatican II ring in our memory. "We must look at war with an entirely new attitude," they said. At the very least this is a call for church leaders, pastoral counselors, and moral theologians not to treat war as an academic question.

Giving Pastoral Counseling a Moral Content

Remember Hans Jägerstätter, the young Austrian Catholic who took seriously the word of Christ, refusing to be inducted for war service? The disturbing element of his story was that he could not find support from his pastors. There is this curious scandal of nationalism that creeps into the church—when the young people who take church teaching most seriously are sometimes the ones who cannot find a comfortable home in our churches.

No, pastoral counseling on draft options, if it is to be faithful to recent teaching, cannot live in a moral vacuum. Pastoral counseling is not to impose—true, but in not being authoritarian, it does not thereby abdicate a wisdom to be handed on. In every other area of morality, the church is not so laissez-faire. How often we hear that it is not only conscience that is significant, but an informed conscience. At the very least, then, our pastoral posture should communicate the unacceptability of participation in any acts "aimed indiscriminately at the destruction of entire cities or of extensive areas along with their population. . . ."

A New Application of Just War Can Lead to Gospel

I have largely stayed with the categories of just-war tradition. Spiritually this tradition has limitations. We must remember that it was not Jesus but Cicero who first gave us this wisdom. And yet the teaching has its value. Today the church has its own way of transforming it—even so far as to show how its true application today makes war "irrational" as a means of vindicating rights. Its application led the World Synod of Bishops (1971) to say that "it is absolutely necessary that international conflicts should not be settled by war" and that a "strategy of nonviolence" is to be fostered. In this sense, if we as pastors truly apply the Catholic teaching and its tradition of just-war conditions of proportionality, we may be blessedly handing on a teaching that is "not far from the kingdom."

The kingdom of Jesus is beyond the kingdom of the nation-state. Just-war teaching has its own dangerous way of being deformed by nationalistic spirits. It has had for too many centuries and too many wars its own way of sterile nonapplication. For church people to stand back and say in effect that one can choose to go to war or one can be a C.O., and to say this in an abstract way, becomes a fearful academicism. It becomes a strange "neutrality" that is not neutral. Young people are swept away in the atmosphere of war and nationalism, so it is a "neutrality" that subtly blesses the status quo.

Augustine meant the teaching as a minimum way of humanizing an already inhuman situation. But today the teaching church uses the basic rationality and humanity of the teaching as a way out of today's improportionate and unacceptable mode of making war. For us as pastors it is time—past time—to begin to apply this teaching at every level. At the diocesan and parish levels let there be a pastoral counseling—indeed a draft counseling—that is faithful to this teaching.

11

Disarmament in the Real World

"Come into the real world!" In discussions on disarmament
how often have we heard that slogan? Events in Iran and
Afghanistan in 1979 and after have sharpened the dilemmas
imposed by the slogan. Thankfully, the events have also provoked within the churches a deeper inquiry into the armaments
issue. I would like here to confine myself largely to the Catholic
context of that discussion by analyzing differing perspectives on
what is the real world. In early 1979, when religious bodies were
being asked to take a position toward SALT II, I began to notice
a curious split in Catholic thinking. The American bishops
through various agencies gave qualified support. But Pax
Christi and some bishops chose not to support it, at least unless
it were radically amended.

The differences then and now are not between right and left,
not between hawk and dove; they are more subtle. All labels will
oversimplify, but for the sake of a handle I would like to name
one side "activist" and the other "liberal." By activist, I mean
the people who tend toward some form of direct action such as
leafletting, demonstrating, holding prayer vigils for peace, etc.
They generally have made disarmament a life priority and often
affiliate with groups such as Pax Christi, the Catholic Peace
Fellowship, or secular peace groups. By liberal, I mean those
who are generally articulate in disarmament issues and who, in
their work for peace, tend toward educational channels. They
will seek to influence events through customary political and
staff processes. Very often the pressure of wide involvements
will impede the liberal from bringing quite the specialized and

concentrated commitment of time and energy that the activist brings to the issue.

Between liberals and activists I have noticed growing tension. In the broadest terms, the activist often sees the liberal as diluting a more gospel witness, and the liberal, in turn, is often miffed at what he or she feels are unrealistic forms of discourse among activists. I would like to isolate three factors that enter into the tension: first, the differing weight given to deterrence; second, a differing methodology; and finally, the problem of concreteness.

In all of this, I know I write not as an impartial observer. For while I do try to articulate here certain reconciling dimensions of the activist vs. liberal tension, nevertheless I clearly do come down on the side of the activist. I do so somewhat unapologetically, since I believe that, in issues of life and death, there can be a form of detached neutrality that muffles all sentiments of moral dread. This in its own way can disguise and distort the enormity of what is at stake. Balanced debating under the guise of neutrality sometimes by its very analytic detachment ends in affirming the reigning praxis. So, I am trying here to avoid that academicism that blesses America's reigning militarism. I know that this kind of conviction carries its own risk of bias, of unfair categories and hidden assumptions. I hope ensuing theological discussion will right any wrongs.

The Three Factors in the Tension

1. Deterrence: One key source of misunderstanding between activist and liberal lies in their differing approaches to deterrence. Liberals generally give more weight to its value, at least as far as explicit articulation goes. They fear certain unrealism in any condemnations that neglect the honest distinction between building weapons for use and building weapons for deterrence. On the other hand, activists fear that the claim of deterrence-motivation becomes a rationalization hiding the inherent dynamism toward use of the weapon no matter what the individualistic assessments of intentionality may be. Activists also fear that Catholic liberals lend legitimacy to nation-state ideologies by their implicit blessing of balance-of-power competitions.

Official Catholic teaching has not generally resolved the argument. So when the activist uses quotations that seem to suppose that it has been resolved, the liberal is doubly vexed. For example, Vatican II condemns the "destruction of entire cities." But the fathers give a classic slide-away when it comes to deterrence: "Whatever be the case with this method of deterrence, men should be convinced that the arms race is not a safe way to preserve a steady peace." So, to the question, Is it a sin to build a nuclear weapon? the church acknowledges a fundamental ambiguity: If it is for use, yes, it is a sin. But the church does not clearly answer the deterrence issue. For a moment let us pass over the Platonic mode of thought that so easily separates human intentions from the systems that are set loose in human history by the very existence of the weapons. Technologies have a life of their own beyond human intentions.

In an authoritative article, James Dougherty synthesizes several decades of documentation: ". . . the church persistently warns the nations not to carry their security apprehensions so far as to fuel the military technology competition to the point of madness."[1] There is implicit here a grudging acceptance of the value of deterrence. So, no matter how indiscriminate or inhumane a weapon may be, the liberal can always find some ambiguity in assessing the morality of its preparation.

This does not mean that Catholic teaching does not provide any material for condemnation. There is the question of degree, the "point of madness." There is also a very serious condemnation of the arms race because of the squandering of money and resources. My main point here, however, is that the official Catholic admission that deterrence does have a limited value manages to deprive Catholic teaching of the clear and unequivocal condemnation of weapons-building. Thus it also impedes consensus in moral evaluation.

There are exceptional places in Catholic teaching where the ambiguity of deterrence does not block a more straightforward condemnation. A striking example is contained in the American bishops' moral teaching, "To Live in Christ Jesus." They proclaim that "not only is it wrong to attack civilian populations, but it is also wrong to threaten to attack them as part of a strategy of deterrence." Such an unequivocal statement goes beyond

Vatican II and even beyond *Pacem in Terris.* Was its issuance a happenstance of committee maneuvering or a genuine development of doctrine from a Spirit-filled assembly? I believe the latter, but at least this can be said: if the words are ever to be taken at face value, then they could open up the weapons industries. If bishops were ever to give this statement a thorough pastoral follow-through, Catholic witness on the arms race could parallel the official witness against abortion, a parallel long earnestly desired by many.

2. *Differing Methodology:* Regardless of authoritative documents, liberals and activists will continue to accent the issue of deterrence differently. Some of that undoubtedly can be ascribed to the pastoral context out of which we speak. This brings us to methodology. In such a vital pastoral question as armaments, there are as many different methods brought to bear as there are people. To attempt to isolate trends is doubly hazardous, but it may clarify the discussion if I name at least two different ways in which the moral sources of human reasoning and Scripture are utilized in discussion.

In broad terms the liberal often speaks out of a more rational Catholic tradition, whereas the activist tends to use a more scriptural language. The activist's pacifism will have a gospel tonality to it. However, Catholic pacifists are rarely purists. Most would "defend their sister from the rapist." Many sense the need for some police power; and most, if they happened upon "the traveler being robbed before the good Samaritan arrived," would probably use some physical force, if necessary, to ward off the attacker. Catholic pacifists have a certain elasticity that moves beyond individualist paradigms in order to encompass social reality. Their gospel language is refreshingly free of fundamentalism, and they do seem capable of dialogue with the more rational categories, such as just-war teaching and the issue of proportionality.

The liberals for their part, while using rational categories, do not thereby place themselves in opposition to gospel simplicity, nor do they necessarily neglect the foolishness of the cross. Many of them, in fact, have reached forms of pacifism through the creation gifts of reasoning and analysis. Thus many recognize modern weaponry's indiscriminate and improportionate destruction. I am trying to be fair in profiling two tendencies that both in Catholic theology and in actual fact are not necessarily opposed. But this does not mean that there is sweet harmony. The dialogue, for example, between members of Pax Christi and members of the United States Catholic Conference (USCC) staff manifests considerable tension.

A typical example of an emphasis on human categories can be found in recent testimony of the USCC before the House Armed Services Committee. The Rev. Bryan Hehir, who heads the Catholic Justice and Peace Office, told the congressmen and women that the "moral principles concerning war and peace . . . have been articulated in a series of works reaching from Augustine's *City of God* through the address of John Paul II at the United Nations last October [1979]." I do not think it is being captious here to note that the first three centuries of the Christian era are lopped off.

No doubt, if Father Hehir were pressed, he would respond that the first three centuries are contained eminently in his thought, that he was speaking in a specific context to a specific problem, which the human categories since Augustine were especially adept at articulating. Even if his Realpolitik slip was showing a little, his audience and his pastoral role of dialogue with the world of honest political realities surely has something to do with emphasis. I have no quarrel with this realism as far as it goes. The question the activist asks, however, is: When does such realism become absorbed in the militarists's own ground of reasoning?

To what degree is our dialogue with the world subverted by the sinful situation that envelops us? A Catholic trusts in creation, yes, but the activists see perhaps more clearly than the liberal how creation has been "subject to futility." This leads to more than methodological tension. The differences become substantive. The liberal becomes annoyed when his dialogue is labeled as futile and compromising, and he feels that the activists' simplicity is sectarian and ultimately isolating and inward. In all of this, while not shrinking from the hard and substantive struggles with one another, we will also have to accord respect and latitude for the way in which different churchly roles and charisms will always lead to different vocabularies and emphases.

3. The Problem of Concreteness: Dealing with different methods and with differing perspectives on deterrence accounts for some of the disagreements among us. But now we come to what I believe is the heart of the matter, namely, the necessity for concreteness in the application of principles. Here I beg the readers' indulgence in allowing my expression of personal conviction that it is the activist who lays hold of the *kairos* and announces a desperately needed orthopraxis.

But before drawing out this conviction, in fairness it needs pointing out that the activists have their way of sinning through abstraction also. Because they do not always have to dialogue with concrete executive decisions of government or industry, there could be a tendency to skirt too easily the complexity of the day-to-day handling of a sinful history's impact on worldly institutions.

The question posed by Reinhold Niebuhr in the 1930s, as to how a group's response to gospel value might not be identical to the individual's response, is a question that time has not washed away. Niebuhrian realism admittedly has been invoked to justify too many abuses of American chauvinism over the years, but at least it does make us face the fact that the transformation of economic and social structures can be more complicated than individual conversion. Indeed, it has been a certain Catholic genius through the centuries to allow that history imposes limits on our well-being and well-doing, and that doing the best one can in a grievous social situation is not always a sinful diluting of gospel values. So peace activists can be unfairly abstract in what they demand here and now, since they are not forced to grapple with some fairly impossible management dilemmas.

The Liberal's Sin of Abstraction

If one has to choose which sin of abstraction is more dangerous and more cosmic in its evil effects, I believe it is the liberal's. It is difficult to avoid suspicion that despite the Catholic effort to impart a vigorous peace morality, somehow there seems to be little concrete application. Too often one misses the here-and-now criticism, of this weapon being made at this time and this place. After the theory is stated, then somehow all things are debatable or left to silence. Recently I came across a classic historical example in an interview conducted by *Sojourners* magazine with the Rev. George Zabelka.[2]

Father Zabelka was the Catholic chaplain of the 509th Composite Air Force Group in August 1945. The 509th was the atomic bomb group, and Tinian Island where he was stationed was the take-off point for the saturation bombings of Japan.

In the interview he admits to knowing better than most that civilians were being killed and not merely "incidentally" or *per accidens*. Why did he not protest? He answers: "I was told it was necessary: told openly by the military and told implicitly by my church's leadership." He continues with a clear description of how structures of the secular, religious, and military society told him clearly that it was all right to "let the Japs have it. . . . The day-in-day-out operation of the state and the church between 1940 and 1945 spoke more clearly about Christian attitudes toward enemies and war than St. Augustine or St. Thomas Aquinas ever could. . . . The question of its morality never seriously entered my mind. I was 'brainwashed' not by force or torture but by my church's silence and wholehearted cooperation in thousands of little ways with the country's war machine."

He then remarks incisively: "I am sure there are church documents around someplace bemoaning civilian death in modern war, and I am sure those in power in the church will drag them out to show that it was giving moral leadership during World War II to its membership."

Is today any different? While we draft our documents, do we not also cooperate in a thousand little ways with the country's war machine? Our people are left blithely unaware of the teachings anyway, and no implications are ever spelled out for specific weapons, for the economy, for taxes, for armaments employment, for ROTC training programs.

Allow me to choose specific examples. The USCC's administrative board in congressional testimony gave qualified support to SALT II. One qualification was well-spoken by Cardinal Krol: "It would radically distort our intentions and purpose if our support of SALT II were in any way coupled with plans for new military expenditures." In the abstract, this may have been a careful realism. But less than a year later the bishops' support was in fact coupled with exorbitant military expenditures when the president announced plans to move toward the MX missile. In the concrete, there was no monitoring of this, nor any sustained protest. Thus the moral qualification becomes an abstract word lost in the shuffle of runaway systems.

Similarly there are stirring church statements on the injury done to the poor by the arms race. Vatican II proclaimed that the arms race "injures the poor to an intolerable degree." And the Holy See's 1976 statement to the United Nations affirms that it "is an act of aggression," for "by their cost alone they kill the poor by causing them to starve." But, in the concrete, when the MX is endorsed by the U.S. Democratic party and set in motion by the president, no outrage is forthcoming from church leadership. It seems that the injury done to the poor in the concrete is quite "tolerable."

The Real Distinction between Liberal and Activist

My suggestion is that the real tension between the liberal and the activist is less due to differing postures toward deterrence, less due to differing methodologies, and more due to judgments about concrete realities and about how desperate and urgent the situation really is. As I see it, it is not that activists are sectarian in their pacifism, not that they shun natural-law or just-war categories or balance-of-power calculations. Rather, they simply wish to know: When will the moral principles emerging from these categories be applied? If bishops and popes can call the arms race a madness, then is there ever a constitutive part of that race that can be named madness too?

When the Congress, in September 1980, appropriates $3.2 million for binary nerve gas preparations, there is no outcry. When Presidential Directive No. 59 canonizes counterforce strategies bringing us closer to first-strike temptations and into a "near occasion" of a "limited nuclear war" (estimates of deaths range in millions for these "limited exchanges"), the only outcry from leadership is polite demurring buried in obscure bureaucratic documents.

When some such as the Berrigans and their friends attempt to say a concrete word to a specific company such as General Electric and when they attempt to say that word loudly and seriously, the only response from liberal leadership seems to be a form of silent disavowal or at best an Olympian tolerance, and this even though the claim against G.E. weaponry would seem to be supported by church teaching. At the challenge of the concrete everything suddenly becomes too complicated for anyone to take a clear position.

In the face of this kind of academicism, the activist has simply nowhere to go except to the gospel. All the rational words have been used and used correctly, but they simply lack the power to seize any *kairos*. The activist's use of the gospel categories is less aimed at a new content and becomes more a liberation from the systematic evasiveness and lethargy that seems to overcome us when it gets down to the nitty gritty. The gospel vocabulary and method then become not a fundamentalist source to skirt complexities of the "real world," but a source of grace and power to sustain the suffering inevitably heaped upon those who confront the real world of a militarist culture.

Whom will history judge to have confronted the real world? In a world where 500 million people (the minimum estimates of the World Bank) are seriously underfed, we build Trident submarines at over a billion dollars apiece, so that we can add fourteen of them to the 2,055 missiles and planes that can launch 9,200 nuclear weapons, each of which is many times more powerful than the Hiroshima weapon.[3]

In this kind of a sin-situation, who is the realist? One looks at lonely persons walking in protest in front of the Pentagon quoting the Sermon on the Mount. Are they sectarian anti-intellectuals? Or have they simply worked their way through the most penetrating analyses of church and state in America, of church and business in America, and come out on the side not of the simplistic but of the true and simple?

One need not be a Latin American theologian to recognize how lack of concrete application in a context of radical urgency, where there is little or no neutral ground, can unwittingly bless the militarist systems that exist. American Catholics ask questions of realism such as: "What do you want us to do when Russia invades countries?" I do not deny the realism and the real problem of power in the world. But the word "us" in the question is significant. The word "us" most often seems to designate one's national identity rather than the deeper identity that we share in Christ the Lord. In fact, Catholic teaching on peace asks us to transcend nation-state identity and reminds us of our common humanity. Yet somehow when push comes to shove, our concrete complicities and loyalties constitute a strange heteropraxis that bestows allegiance on the idol of a national security ideology.

I do not mean here to cast stones at liberals or anyone who works through educational or staff channels. Given my own work as a teacher, I would indeed be living in a glass house. It is important also to remember that my categories of liberal and activist are artificial and too broad to cover the many degrees of each and the mutual movement between them. I have simply utilized the categories in order to emphasize especially the issue of the concrete. Ultimately it will never be a question of either/or, but of both/and. If activism is to escape charges of an unhealthy elitism, it must always seek ways of networking and coalition-building with broader constituencies. So, in praising the activist I am not anxious to impose one form of witness or universalize one special charism. Each charism is for the other. Each will be looking for ways not to exclude the other but to invite one another to "come and see" the truth and insight they have found.

I am holding up the activist's instinct for the meaning of the concrete as a special theological source of wisdom and insight for the whole church. This does not mean everyone must immediately become activist in the same way. But activist and liberal can work together listening to and utilizing each other's wisdom. Thomas Merton once wrote that "the insanity of the arms race had the approbation of a schizoid military and business complex and . . . schizoid religious sects." In the face of the militarist systems presently at work in America and the world and in the face of the seemingly calm consent of many American Catholics, it seems one role of a theologian, in order to avoid the occupational hazard of becoming schizoid, is to raise an anxious voice about the concrete urgency of the situation. I express regret if in so doing I have in any way caricatured others' thoughts or missed the value of their unique and special contribution to the church's witness for peace.

12

Making the Connection between
Sexual Ethics and Social Justice

From the 1960s on there has been much development in
Catholic thought on sexuality. There has also been not a little
criticism of the Catholic past. Most adult Catholic's today grew
up in a church in which there was, to borrow words from psy-
chologist Eugene Kennedy, "more than sufficient guilt in the
room." Michael Harrington, in his *Fragments of a Century,*
satirized the Catholic past by noting the difference in assessing
the degree of sinfulness in the area of alcohol consumption as
opposed to sexuality. He noted with tongue in cheek and with
some ethnic self-deprecation that the greater latitude given to
alcohol might have signaled the measure of Irish dominance in
the American Catholic church.

This is not to throw out the baby with the bathwater. Past
teaching did contain the high ground of a constant and gifted
instinct for sexuality as a vehicle of loving self-donation in marriage. The task of the contemporary church is to see that our
reaction to the past is healthy and discerning lest we replace the
tyranny of a past superego with the no less tyrannical demands
of a new libertinism. Harvey Cox was not the first to point out
that the playboy phenomenon of the 1960s was no less a Manichaeanism than the early Puritanism. He wisely suggested at one
point that a figleaf painted over genitals is one problem, but a
figleaf placed over the face of the person's humanity signifies a
demon worse than the first.

Not all has been sweet harmony in the recent past, however.
Controversy has accompanied the before and after periods of

Paul VI's issuance of *Humanae Vitae* as well as the 1977 publication of the study done by the Catholic Theological Society of America, *Human Sexuality*. Allow me to point out one danger in these controversies even as they continue today, namely, that they tend to absorb pastoral energies that could be better utilized elsewhere.

Paul Hanly Furfey is a moral theologian who for decades has been begging church people to begin to *apply* Catholic social teachings to the concrete world. In his inspired writings he taught us how issues of conventional and individual morality managed to preoccupy the church to the neglect of public, moral concerns, which have cried out for more prophetic leadership. Whenever we become concerned with a sexual issue, we would do well to remember that only a few hours' journey away from North America, many priests, religious, and lay people are undergoing imprisonment, danger, torture, even death. They struggle courageously over issues of faith and justice, freedom and food. It would be tragic if the North American churches were seduced again into obsessions with the sexual that easily domesticate the church, privatize its message, and divert its prophetic voice away from critical social judgments crucial to the moral and human well-being of the peoples of the world.

My reflection here is an effort not to allow this to happen. We cannot prevent the church from involving itself in sexual issues. Anything so dense as the sexual is with its significance for human growth has to have salvational implications. And so the sexual will always hold some place for church discussion. One hopes that it will be discerning and compassionate discussion. Our job here is to see to it that while we discern sexual morality, we never forget the full social context.

My real agenda here is to try to communicate what to many may seem a surprise. My overall reflection here is this, that what may seem today to be a conservative sexual teaching is really socially progressive, and the more permissive sexual teaching, I believe, will someday be seen to be socially reactionary in the sense that it tends to ratify an individualistic and consumer society.

I shall go about this reflection in three parts. First, I shall review the central church teaching that marriage is the normative place for sexual behavior; and I shall show why this sexual teaching can have something to do with nurturing a more humane organic community. Second, I shall take the central teaching of the church on the meaning of the sexual as both love and life (unitive and procreative). Here I shall show how the teaching can be socially prophetic. (I shall refrain from entering the polemics surrounding *Humanae Vitae,* regarding the issue of "each and every act." For our purposes, it will be better to stay with the broad lines of thought about love and life. On this there is wide convergence in the church.) Third, I shall propose some ideas for a ministry in the church that would be more balanced in integrating its concerns about the sexual with those of social justice.

The Social Significance of Limiting Sex to Marriage

For some two thousand years the church has taught that sex is to be reserved for marriage. I suspect there is something deeper here than what is usually discussed. I believe that the teaching ultimately is asking for a form of human community that reflects God's faithful love.

But first let us be sure we have some healthy insight into the personalist dimensions of this ethic. Marriage is something more than just "a piece of paper giving permission to live together." The New Testament teaches that a man clinging to his wife is a "two becoming one" in a way that signifies Christ's love for his church. Suppose we take a line of reasoning around just one aspect of marriage and intercourse, namely, the *unitive* aspect. Let me reason in a personalist, step-by-step manner. For example, I say that the very bodily intimacy of sexual love has its own inner way of crying out for *exclusivity*; also, that the very bodily way of "clinging" has an inner way of demanding that we wake up in responsibility for one another on the morning after and indeed on all the mornings after (*fidelity*). Let me go one step further and say that, since the human is a social, public, and ritual being, any love expressed in sexual intercourse cries out to be vowed in public ritual (*ceremonial*). This vowing ends in a *proclamation* that names the deepest divine significance of the human reality, namely, God's love for his people through the death and resurrection of his Son (*sacrament*). In other words, let us take a line of reasoning that helps us to understand that the moral norm of reserving intercourse for marriage is not merely a heteronomous legal norm, but more in the order of a wisdom tradition announcing what intercourse really is at its deepest meaning.

This is a line of reasoning that sees the prohibition of intercourse outside of marriage as an intrinsic implication, a congruous honoring of what intercourse really is. I am asking not a philosophy, but whether or not reserving sexual intercourse to *marriage in the Lord* is a scriptural way of making human realities become a privileged sign of God's loving fidelity in Jesus. Is it not in fact Scripture teaching us how the sexual can become a way of loving as Christ loves us?

But now comes the deeper question. The way Christ loved his people is a *forever* love, even to the point of dying. This has significance for community. My point then is that any movement away from seeing marriage as the normative context for sexual activity is unwittingly nurturing, or at least ratifying, a socioeconomic posture that is conservative rather than progressive. Such a hypothesis would demand a whole book to itself. Here I can only suggest a brief line of inquiry. I also feel obliged to present it less as an assertion and more as a suspicion, as a question for discussion.

Schematically the line of inquiry is basically this: I first point out how a life-affecting ethic nurtures a certain separateness of a religious group. Second, how we interpret being *unworldly* may be influenced by our own "praxis." In other words, how and what we search out in the Scriptures is influenced not only by a philosophy but also by our social position. Third, one meaning of "worldliness" is embracing a consumer capitalism that forces people into an individualism and a form of transient relationships that make it difficult to experience the meaning of fidelity and therefore of God's love for his people.

The New Testament ethic is basically a "communion" (koinonia) ethic. How we live sexually can be a way of helping to bring about the koinonia here and now. Reserving sexual expression for marriage can be a way of affirming a system of organic relationships that can more easily shadow forth that Christ is faithful to his people even unto death.

Juan Luis Segundo, in his *Liberation of Theology,* adapts

Rudolf Bultmann's "hermeneutic circle" to the issue of social status. His key point, as I read him, is this: in the struggle for liberation, "there comes a new way of experiencing theological reality that leads us to exegetical suspicion, that is, to the suspicion that the prevailing interpretation of the Bible has not taken important pieces of data into account."[1] Could this apply to North Atlantic theologians searching the Scriptures with regard to sexuality? Is it possible for North Americans to understand how worldly is the individualism that is endemic to their economic system?

Some sociologists before Marx saw that the rise of industrial capitalism would produce the *Gesellschaft* society, that is, the society where "everybody is by himself and isolated."[2] Is it not possible that the Catholic community itself is at a place on the socioeconomic ladder where systemic individualism becomes a more controlling factor in their imagination than when they lived in more organic, ethnic communities? Marx pressed the idea that the further up the ladder one was, the less one was capable of sensing his or her own alienation. It is possible, then, that even as we search the Scriptures, we are less prepared to hear the ethic that could unmask our own alienation. If this is so, it may be that we are less likely to realize how deep are the sexual ramifications of embracing the individualistic worldliness of our society.

It is as difficult for us to realize the social and cultural context out of which we search Scriptures as it is for a fish to realize that it is in water (Alfred North Whitehead's analogy). Perhaps we could use as an analogy the systemic problem of slavery in the antebellum South. For a slaveowner to dismiss his slaves abruptly could in some cases have been an act of cruelty, so deeply entrenched was the system. Moreover, it would not have been easy for theologians of that time (especially those theologians who would attempt too simple a process of inquiring into the "instinct of the faithful") to understand all the implications of Paul to Philemon or of Paul's forbidding any distinction between "slave and free" (Gal. 3:28).

Can the Catholic imagination today grasp the meaning of the New Testament's vision of living in communion? We live in a culture with little organic community. Relationships are transient and functional. But the New Testament churches tried to live and theologize out of a communion. Even if their life had deficiencies, the vision must remain for us a moral call, an eschatological pull. We must find a way of living over against a worldliness that is individualistic and transient. For in transience there is at stake the theological issue of faithfulness, and faithfulness is at the heart of the plan of salvation.

Sex outside of marriage is in some way understandable, given the terrible, lonely reality of our day. But, in some way, I fear it ratifies the deeper systemic sin. If we examine the Scriptures while living in less-consuming and less-transient communities, perhaps there will be a more fertile ground for receiving insight about reserving sex for marriage. Is it not simply a way of saying that so close a union of bodies must remind people of God's faithful love for his Son's risen body, his church? Then we shall see the New Testament ethic as countercultural not simply because it is more strict (Manichaean), but because it is more richly communitarian. An ethic that reserves sex for marriage may be a way of signifying and nurturing a community of more permanent bonds, a community where we must love one another as Christ loved us, that is, until death. One place where we try to make this happen in a visible way is in marriage.

Connecting the Doctrine on Love and Life with a Progressive Social Teaching

I ask the reader now to look for a second at the church's vision of sexuality as both unitive and procreative. Keep a large heart and do not allow biases or strong feeling on birth-control issues to color your judgment. Remember that even though there is wide disagreement about whether or not the church should forbid contraception in each and every act in a conflict situation, still there is a wide consensus of theologians (even those who dissent from *Humanae Vitae*) that affirms the great synthesis of love and life. It is not just a sexual teaching but a basic anthropological insight that sees that love must have some dynamism outward, must overflow somehow, must have some "superabundance" if it is to remain true love.

This vision is socially prophetic in a way not often communicated. Allow me two examples, showing how the vision can speak: (1) through a more organic effort to solve population issues; (2) through requiring and nurturing hope for the future against a new Manichaean despair.

In the face of world hunger, there have been tendencies among Americans and other developed nations to make "population" the central problem. The impulse to solve the problem becomes, typically, ruled by the technological mindset. Americans seem unaware that the real explosion is not population but the consumption explosion of the developed nations. Paul VI hit the point sharply at the World Food Conference in 1974, saying, "It is inadmissible that those who have control of the wealth and resources of mankind should try to resolve the problem of hunger by forbidding the poor to be born."

The church seems to have had an early insight into a very real population mechanism, namely, that population-decrease comes most effectively through economic development, and that there is something ecologically inhuman and unbalanced for a government to enter forcefully the sanctuary of the family, when economic justice and more organic development are left unattended. This insight of the church is not unconnected with its conviction regarding the respect for both the life and the love dimensions of human sexuality. In other words, instead of reading the church's population analysis as merely an overflow of a sexual "hangup," I am suggesting that there is an ecology built into our sexual ethic that connects the organic demands of being open to life in intercourse with the organic ways of solving world hunger issues. Let us proceed more deeply, then, into the connections between the social and the sexual by a second example.

There is something in the social order that interacts with individual morality. One cannot separate one's feelings about sex from one's feelings about history and humanity. Take, for example, the strong cultural impetus toward sterilization today. In an insightful article, Midge Decter touches on the connection between the social and the sexual. She says: "Look at the willfully childless couple in their early 30's. . . . Both are suffering from a soul-killing lack of responsibility for the future and for someone and something beyond self that . . . is making their lives feel meaningless to them."[3] Her thought here runs deeper than the issue of judging an individual's motives for responsible parenthood. The concern is over a social trend, a lack of self-transcendence, a lack of care for the future. It is a real lack of hope in the world, a deep distrust in the world's goodness, ultimately "the profoundest kind of self-hatred."

The church's teaching is not merely to say what it once had to insist upon against the Manichaeans—that procreation is good because matter is not evil. It *is* saying this, but its insistence that sexuality remain in procreative context also proclaims that the world is a place of hope, that our lives and our selves are worth reproducing.

A similar thought is provoked by Christopher Lasch in his insights into contemporary narcissism.[4] He persuasively argues that narcissism is not only an individual pathology, but the underlying structure of our age. One of his many insights is the way in which easier sex trivializes not only sex, but relationships themselves. Here he extends an idea popularized by Rollo May on how too much erotica will spell the end of that healthy human passion that we call "eros." Lasch makes a key connection for our purposes here, saying that "when sex is for the couples alone, the relationship can be terminated at pleasure." This leads to a "wary avoidance of emotional commitments." And then comes a central thought: the inability to take an interest in anything after one's own death makes intimacy more elusive than ever.

Here again we see the prophetic instinct of church teaching. The church insists that sex is so untrivial that it take place only in a situation of permanency with procreative possibility. The church says relationships are not to be "cool." It implicitly requires a passionate love for the other person, and ultimately for the child who will exist even beyond our death. Correct sex looks for a future. It is no accident that sexual libertinism accompanies social apathy; no accident that the loss of hope of avoiding the bomb should foster sexual mores that escape into the "cabaret" of temporary liaisons.

The church instinct for reserving the sexual for marriage goes more deeply than we had dreamed. It is in the end a prophetic insistence against certain cultural deformations of sexuality, which carry their effects into social realities such as hunger, the threat of the bomb, and for a world worth being passionate about, a world whose future is worth caring about.

Integrating Sexual and Social Concerns in Ministry

We have been exploring ways in which the church's sexual ethic carries a form of social prophecy. For pastors and for the ministry at every level, this yields a new dimension to the role of "watching over" *(episcopos)* the flock, a dimension that I would call an "integral" solicitude. By this I mean that our watchfulness regarding correct sexual teaching touches the deeper layers of social values symbolized by the sexual teachings. Take, for example, three points mentioned earlier, namely, world population, sterilization, and the need for more permanent organic forms of community.

First, in regard to hunger and population, I am thinking of how Indira Gandhi's forced sterility program may have had some roots in the austerity programs imposed upon India through the International Monetary Fund. An integral solicitude in this case, even for Americans, would include an effort not only to safeguard the church's sexual teaching but to attempt to look at the mechanisms of American economic decisions on India. The temptation to force birth control is not unconnected with American economic policies.

Second, take the solicitude required in the issue of sterilization in America. Few other issues have provoked such anxiety among bishops. There have been anxious questions sent to the Vatican on this subject and then lengthy commentaries on Rome's reply. But if sterilization as a social trend has something to do with people sensing the worth of bringing a child into the world, we must be equally exercised over the issues that influence subconscious fears of parents. A minister rightfully speaks against a selfish form of sterilization, but he must also address those matters that cause people to want to be sterilized because of their distrust in the world's future. So, those who speak against sterilization, if they wish to be integral, will speak against companies producing the weaponry that works its sterility at subconscious levels (not to mention the literal sterilization being visited on people through radioactive wastes). I do not intend here just a general *fervorino* encouraging ministers to be vigilant on social issues. Rather, I am suggesting that there is direct and inherent interaction between sexual practices and social practices. The antichild atmosphere is a phenomenon not at all unrelated to a certain form of escape from the future that the nuclear madness subconsciously induces. It is intrinsically connected with whether or not sex is seen as an escape, whether or not the world is a place to escape from, a place definitely not in which to risk having a child. The church's effort to restore a healthy eros includes a judgment against those elements in the milieu that breed an escape from feeling and a passionlessness.

In regard to community, our solicitude against transitory sex includes a care about the very wellsprings of community in the life of the church itself. For example, a priest may exhibit perfect loyalty to the Holy See in sexual teachings, but may be a sign of contradiction in the distant and bureaucratic way he administers the parish community. He ends curiously ratifying at one level what he preaches against at another level. The prophetic teaching that demands a stable marriage for intercourse will be all the more congruent coming out of a church of more permanent human relationships where people can sense the meaning of church as real community.

Today we know better than yesterday how the milieu can subvert the best of our teaching. The pure water of healthy sexual teaching is a gift of God's Spirit to his people. But if the plumbing structure of social relations within and without the household becomes rusty, our best efforts are wasted. The teaching becomes contaminated at every juncture.

So we return to where we began. The church's vision of love and life in human sexuality is based on the intrinsic good of the human community of persons. It is ultimately a public issue. Not to be integral in our concern is to regress to an individualistic morality. This is to allow our voice to be privatized. To be privatized is to be domesticated, to be subtle supporters of the status quo. Many feel this is what happened in Germany. While National Socialism rose to power, too many in the church turned inward. Sex is not only a metaphor for social living, it is also a symbol. A symbol is like a sacrament in that it also contains reality. Integral solicitude attempts to deal with both the *sign* and the *res,* the social reality of both sin and its individual symbol of unchastity, and the social reality of salvation and its individual sacrament of married sexuality.

13

Worship in Spirit and Truth— And Civil Religion

But an hour is coming, and is already here, when authentic worshipers will worship the Father in spirit and truth.
[John 4:23]

From the very beginnings of the Christian church there was a recognition that worship in spirit and truth could be compromised, especially by idolatry toward the temporal ruler. Christians knew instinctively that they could not swing incense to Caesar. And they had to go through the pivotal experience of the New Testament learning that in Christ there was "neither Greek nor Jew" (Gal. 3:28).

There is something about Christianity that is always bursting the bonds of our *belongings*. In some way we are asked to move beyond family, beyond tribe, beyond nation. We belong to God. And yet all of these are parts of God's creation and therefore good. In this chapter I would like to examine this paradox so that our social criticism of America will rest on solid moral and dogmatic ground. Allow me to begin in an unexpected place: the Baltimore Catechism.

The Fourth Commandment's Ambiguity

The catechism says that we "are obliged to respect and to obey legitimate civil authority" and that a citizen "must love his country. . . and respect and obey lawful authority." The catechism, of course, allows citizens to "defend themselves against tyranny," and insists that the authority be lawful.

When the catechism was written there did not seem to be much tension between love of country and love of God. One did not ask then how *much* one could love country and still love God. Yet the question *has* been asked through the ages. There has always been some tension to be worked out. The tension is illustrated by two texts of the apostolic church. One affirms that "there is no authority except from God . . ." (Rom. 13:1). The other gives us the apostles' words of resistance: "Better for us to obey God than men" (Acts 5:29).

Why is this question so important for our times? Why is it especially important for Christians living in America? The answer seems to be contained in the way many moral issues now present themselves with social and international dimensions.

There is a certain advantage in talking about this issue under the rubric of the Fourth Commandment. The older moral manuals did so and they included under the one virtue of *pietas* both the reverence due to parents and our duties toward our country. Yet even here there was a tension. For the moral manuals also handled the issue of when obedience would not be required and when resistance would be necessary.

In these sections of the manuals the analogy with the family is never far absent. The Christian tradition has always had a sense of the ambivalence of family love. Moreover, in the vocation literature as well as in our hagiography there has always been a sense of how the gospel relativizes the reverence due to parents. There is some way of leaving family for the sake of the gospel (cf. Mk. 10:29).

This tradition can serve us well. It has a certain simplicity. And the psychology involved in issues of both family and state resistance can be similar enough to be spiritually comparable. The cutting of unhealthy family ties is not dissimilar to the psychology and spirituality necessary for that critical distance that we must sometimes bring to the policies of the nation-state.

In our day we have better control of the psychological implications involved here. I am talking about the freedom from a tyrannical superego that allows for a mature love toward country as well as toward parents. This more authentic and mature "piety" allows for distance, for criticism, for recognition of evil, for ambivalent feelings. The false "piety" of superego arises from primitive needs of approval and necessarily represses any awareness of imperfection in parent or country.

There is much to be said about these psychological issues. My purpose here is only to allude to them in order to suggest that the more mature our spirituality and the more mature our Catholic formation, then the more freedom and greater critical sense will Catholics be able to bring to national policies on such issues as hunger and disarmament.

Civil Religion

In any discussion today of religious attitudes toward one's country, it will be well to consider a sociological phenomenon that comes under the heading "civil religion." The term is used in different senses and it is not always easy to pin down exactly what is meant. I would like to mention two uses of the term that are theologically significant for basing a social critique of America.

The first and most central meaning of "civil religion" is a pejorative one. It sees faith as being totally absorbed into the culture of the nation. Faith no longer discloses the transcendent God but is simply a function of belonging to the American culture. Faith is exploited for the needs of civil society. The religion is no longer truly Jewish, truly Protestant, truly Catholic. It has become American. Will Herberg's famous work *Protestant-Catholic-Jew*, first published in 1955, is an example of this understanding. At the time he was reflecting on the ambivalence of the postwar religious revival.

While he did not use the exact term "civil religion," he had equivalent words. He called it, for example, a "religiousness without religion" in which the notion of "standing 'over against' the world is deeply repugnant."[1] This form of civil religion, while perhaps still rooted in prophetic tradition, emerges as the opposite of that tradition, and the religious person "simply cannot understand an Elijah or an Amos, a Jesus or an Isaiah."[2] He calls it an "American culture-religion," a "fusion of religion with national purpose" that "passes over into the direct exploitation of religion for economic and political ends."[3]

This meaning of civil religion is certainly the dominant theme of Marie Augusta Neal's collection of articles entitled *A Socio-Theology of Letting Go*.[4] With a good deal of nuance she documents both the mechanisms of civil religion and its impact on America's structural relations to problems of world poverty. Her anecdote about a special session of the United Nations General Assembly is a telling one. The meeting occurred on May 1, 1974, and concerned third world proposals on the New International Economic Order and on issues of trade and pricing. Later she had a meeting with an organization of Christian media people, who represented some twenty-nine denominations. When she asked what coverage they would give this meeting of the United Nations General Assembly, only five people even knew of its occurrence. All anecdotes limp, but this one does illustrate Herberg's insights into how the different faiths, when they are face to face with national policies, can lose their distinctive impact.

It goes without saying, then, that this form of civil religion encourages an uncritical form of obedience and reverence for the homeland. Religious images become sources of a new idolatry, spinning out a specious form of Fourth Commandment loyalty. It is a kind of impious piety that loses the transcendence of God and no longer worships in spirit and truth.

This idolatry happens in unintended ways often hidden from the worshipers' conscious eyes. In fact sometimes it happens under the guise of the highest motives—indeed even religious motives. José Comblin, writing of various situations in Latin America, details the way in which "national security" becomes an ideology that attempts to make coalition with the church.[5] While this example is taken from Latin American sources, it is still helpful to North Americans to be awakened to how a value such as national security can be demonic in its power and insidiousness for any country. We begin to do things like bless bombers that will drop atom bombs on civilians in Nagasaki and Hiroshima, and thus our worship is no longer offered to the God who transcends national boundaries.

Civil Religion as Ideals and a Dream

The second meaning that the term "civil religion" carries tends to be more neutral and nuanced. Robert Bellah, in his 1975 study *The Broken Covenant*, defined it as "that religious dimen-sion, found . . . in the life of every people, through which it interprets its historical experience in the light of transcendent reality."[6] The Pilgrims, of course, saw themselves as a chosen people, a New Israel having crossed the equivalent of the Red Sea into the land given them by the Lord. In this sense civil reli-gion uses religious themes to explain both America's origins and its destiny.

The important point here is that Bellah sees in the civil religion certain transcendent dimensions that allow for prophetic judg-ment. In this sense the civil religion, instead of being a force that only co-opts the prophetic voice, instead of simply dulling peo-ple into a complacency that endorses the status quo, becomes in history a force for renewal. The example par excellence is con-tained in Lincoln's Second Inaugural Address where the Civil War is seen as God's punishment for America's going against its own dream in its enslavement of the black man and woman.

Notice then that here civil religion takes on a curious twist. America's dream is used to judge America's failure. It contains within itself a prophetic and transcendent dimension. America sees itself as a covenanted people and then is able to be called to judgment for its "broken covenant."

This has important implications for religious leaders, who must speak a prophetic word on issues of hunger and arms if our worship is to be in spirit and truth.

The Theological Implication of the Ambiguity of Civil Religion

There is a theological importance in social concerns, namely, not to lose some sense of goodness in the world. I am not talking here of a kind of false optimism that may have characterized a certain form of liberalism in the 1960s, but of a basic theological posture.

There is a way in which the best-intentioned social critic may subtly fall into a new Manichaeanism or Jansenism. Some radi-cal social critics may start out concerned about the world, but end up so countercultural as to lose all possibility of seeing goodness or using goodness in social structures. H. Richard Niebuhr's words are applicable here: "At the edges of the radical movement the Manichean heresy is always developing."[7] We can avoid such Manichaeanism by recognizing that there are some transcendent and prophetic impulses in the nation's dream and its ideals.

Theologically, then, it is a recognition that the grace of Christ is found beyond the church. It can even be found in some way in civic ideals and public structures. The fathers of the church kept this theology in view. When they considered how the pagans could also be virtuous and enlightened, they then speculated that the Word of God even before the incarnation had spread God's seeds beyond the church and beyond the Christian faith.[8]

Thomas Clark has popularized this thought as applied to social structures. He teaches that we must recognize that not only sin but also grace becomes entrenched in structures and systems.[9] In other words, the modern pastor has become somewhat sophisticated in his or her recognition that evil is structural and systemic and not merely *individual* sin. But we must become conscienticized not only as to how we are oppressed but also as to how we have been blessed structurally. Thus Bellah's clarification of civil religion as an ambivalent phenomenon can push the social critic to more vigorous, responsible discernment. He or she must make an enlightened, careful effort to find, uncover, recognize, and name structures and dimensions of national policies and public practices that may carry the "seeds of the Logos" or have a potential for redemption.

The Pastoral Advantage of Ambiguity

In a work on Thomas Merton, James Finley remarked humorously that every prophet may be a pain in the neck, but not every pain in the neck is a prophet.[10] There is a certain graciousness in those who keep a sense of how the world contains both good *and* bad institutions. But even more to the point, we are forced to be more judicious in our social criticism. The prophetic impact is dulled when its message is too sweeping or when it offers only moral exhortation to the will, with no data for the intellect. Moralism takes the place of moral judgment. Passion without facts. Words that do not discern data twist what could have been an authentic moral insight into mere political demagoguery.

Even in socially oriented homilies there is need for a sense of a "good news." Homilies are not to be ethical exhortations only— no matter how enlightened. There is the proclamation of gift. Social concern is more Christian when it comes out of thanksgiving. John Langan, in his advice on utilizing the insights of liberation theology in North America, suggests that the North American middle class will have difficulty identifying themselves as oppressors.[11] Honoring this instinct may not necessarily be a "watering down." And it may be more than diplomacy. It may have a truthful theological basis in the reality of North America. An analogy may illustrate here. In the thirty-day retreat it was Ignatius's genius to bring the retreatant to a deeper sense of guilt by first realizing his creational gifts and, above all, how beloved he was of God. So also in our preaching on national social issues, by using Robert Bellah's insights into the goodness of some American dreams and ideals, we may be allowing the listener the very security needed to sense the depth of America's national corruption.

If this hope is not to be twisted, there is one important caution. We must recognize that the good values found in the nation or its structures are good not because they are of the nation, but because they are of God. Jürgen Moltmann says this with greater perceptiveness. After speaking of the greatness of the dream of "freedom, equality and happiness" contained in the Declaration of Independence, he goes on to caution us to recognize this not as an *American* dream but as a *human* dream. Indeed, he points out what happens when we miss this point:

> The human dream cannot be Americanized without being falsified through the ideological self-justification of the American empire and the free enterprise of the multinational corporations. As a human dream, the American dream is a true and necessary one. As an American dream, however, it makes the human dream impossible.[12]

Moltmann goes on to explain that there is promise in some of America's messianism and apocalypticism but only if they are Christianized—and this involves sacrifice. "Without readiness for sacrifice America remains an ambiguous promise."[13] I point out these insights of Moltmann simply to caution that even the positive elements in American civil religion cannot go unqualified.

A Mature Spirituality

Christopher Mooney, in *Religion and the American Dream*, utilizes William Lee Miller's famous phrase for expressing healthy ambivalent feelings toward one's country: "Of thee, nevertheless, I sing." The symbol combines an intense criticism with intense patriotism. And this can be the mark of a more mature spirituality. There is in our worship a need for "singing, nevertheless." That is, we sing our praise amid the recognition of evil. We are not the church of the perfect, but of the poor. Worship in spirit and truth keeps both grace and sin in awareness. We sing, "Lord have mercy" and "Glory to God."

There is an irony in that the one who has become too dour and too pessimistic toward the nation has subtly allowed the evildoer to co-opt the nation. In Israel the prophets did not lose the sense of their roots. They were the patriots, not the king. In an earlier chapter I alluded to the example of Thomas More. He never lost his almost primordial sense of loyalty. He was the "King's good servant"—more so than those who had signed the Oath of Supremacy, and he knew it. There is something deep here that keeps trust in God, just as there is something demonic in the nihilist no matter how moral and prophetic his or her cause may be.

Even more significantly in spiritual terms, one who holds to the goodness of one's roots can often preserve oneself from forms of illusion. The grass is not always greener outside the national boundaries. Daniel Berrigan makes this point with striking humility in talking about his own movement away from a certain naiveté regarding the North Vietnamese.

I remember a comment by Peter Berger in *Rumor of Angels*. He pokes a good-humored if unfair quip at the tendency of Catholic priests who, upon their social awakening, suddenly rush headlong into Marxism.

Spiritually, then, to be able to sing about the nation with a certain sense of the "nevertheless" does not diminish one's criticism, but may even intensify it. Indeed, as Bellah points out, in the very singing of certain national songs there is a recall to the prophetic dream. So we sing in "Battle Hymn of the Republic" that "He is trampling out the vintage where the grapes of wrath are stored." The hymn provided the title for one of the twentieth-century's greatest novels of social protest.

So the two meanings of civil religion can be held together. The god of civil religion is not the god to worship, and yet in some dimensions of the created human enterprise one can find the image of God.

Conclusion

What are we commanded by the Fourth Commandment? To love our country, yes. But also to criticize and resist: to speak the word that builds up and to speak the word that tears down. The virtue of *pietas* is an adult virtue. The Christian vocation will always ask us, as Abraham was asked, in some way to leave a homeland for a land that God will show us. No wonder that Dom Helder Camara begs North Americans to become "Abrahamic minorities."

There is a sound theological anthropology at the base of healthy social criticism of one's country. It recognizes both sin and grace in the country and sin and grace in the church. It does not deny the potential for total corruption, but it does recognize goodness at origins and in dreams. There is a nonviolent sense of redeemability.

As Christians we avoid the nationalism that unites God and country too easily. But we also avoid the dualistic tendency that radicals sometimes slip into, separating God and country too easily. For we know that the nation in its dreams and images and symbols can contain the "seeds of the Logos." In that sense we not only bring the presence of Christ to the nation through our prophetic criticism, but also uncover the presence of Christ in unexpected places. Jesus said to the Samaritan woman that it was "neither on this mountain nor in Jerusalem" that we would worship in spirit and truth. Ultimately, when all is said and done, we must worship the living God, and not the nation-state.

Epilogue: The Growing Urgency

The chapters in this book represent a journey of my own—an intellectual journey, and yet more than that; a journey, I hope, of grace and the heart.

It may help the reader to tie the foregoing chapters together if I speak of some recent gifts of the journey as they throw light on what has been said above.

The Horizontal and the Vertical

In the beginning of the book I spoke of the paradox of the horizontal and the vertical. By that I meant that Jesus gave glory to his Father (vertical) at the very moment he laid down his life for his brothers and sisters (horizontal). He is raised up in resurrection at the very moment he embraces the world and forgives the world. The deepest act of his humanity, the laying down of his life for us, is an epiphany for us of his divine Sonship.

I think that the very beginnings of my own training as a moral theologian opened my mind to this idea. I can remember this point being made by my teachers at the Alfonsianum in Rome and by various lectures during those exciting Vatican Council days from 1962 to 1965. But as time goes on, this truth becomes more and more apparent. Worship in spirit and truth, as we have said throughout these chapters, is nurtured by going out to the other, to the poor. One cannot help but see how even bishops and priests as they move among those who are poor begin to drop false concerns, false modes of interacting with their people. One is reminded of Saul on the way to Damascus. He meets along the way the poor Christ, and the bonds of his narrow world are burst. I see seminarians encounter the poor, and suddenly some of the clericalisms disappear. A certain false "churchiness"

vanishes and their spirituality begins to flourish in a real
open-hearted, gifted humility and fraternity. I believe their
prayer life becomes more real and more authentic.

Structures for Life and Peace-Justice

The prologue of this book lays an emphasis on structural
work for justice, an emphasis that perdures throughout the
book. We have gone beyond a social thought that deals only in
interpersonal forms of honesty. After the Enlightenment, care
for our brothers and sisters must assume a stewardship over
systems and public institutions.

I have tried to apply this to the issue of abortion, and even to
sexuality itself. What often passes for liberal opinions in these
areas are, in reality, socially regressive. In other words, abortion
and easier sex tend to ratify an individualistic consumerism that
ultimately splits people apart, not to mention the killing of the
weak.

There is in my own life something that links the chapters on
abortion and sexuality in this book, and those on peace, Eucharist, and concern for the poor. The link can be explained this
way: in the past few years I have had one foot in the peace movement and one foot in the pro-life movement. And more and
more the absurdity of separating these issues is becoming apparent. I have tasted in an inner way the coherence between the
two concerns. When I link the issue of anti-abortion with disarmament and with international justice, I am not simply trying
to be clever in my argument.

Allow me to illustrate one aspect of this experiential learning
about the coherence of pro-life and pro-peace. I have noticed
when lecturing against abortion how people sometimes evade
issues. They skip away from an insight by running to a safe
point; and then run from one slogan to another. Finally they end
up using subtle (and not so subtle) epithets such as "right-wing
pro-lifers" or "anti-abortion zealots." One evades issues by
lumping people together under the most absurd banners. Then I
started to notice the very same phenomenon when I lectured on
disarmament. Tags such as "zealot" and "unbalanced" are applied to those who tend to be seriously concerned. "Straw men"

are set up so they can be easily argued against. People argue against the Berrigans by "setting them up"; they make it seem, for example, that activists are necessarily for "total unlimited disarmament," and, of course, one can then formulate what amounts to a demagogic appeal against such "unrealism." In both issues there is an unwillingness to look at concrete realities such as the child in the womb and the child injured by bombs.

Marxism as a Label

For years now in Latin America any priest, Sister, or lay leader who has a serious care for the poor is labeled "Marxist" or—and this is becoming a favorite phrase—"an unwitting tool of the Marxists." Maryknoll priests are defamed; the Jesuit order is labeled as pink; Sisters who did nothing but try to help refugees are smeared as "gun-runners" or "maybe running a roadblock," in order somehow to rationalize murder. In Latin America this is not just an intellectual game. People are killed because of such slanders. Torture is rationalized, by people who profess to be Christians, on the grounds of "national security."

There is a common pattern whenever one begins to speak in behalf of the weak, whether for the unseen child of the womb or the unseen children of the third world. One must be prepared to meet with evasion, caricature, labeling, and, in some countries, downright persecution. In fact, the whole business of seeing communist subversion beneath every Latin American struggle obscures the real issues. The real issues, when the history of America is retold, may not at all be a history of East vs. West, or of communism vs. capitalism, or of atheistic Russia vs. the Christian West. Merton as far back as 1961 saw that some would "calculate how, by a 'first strike,' the glorious Christian West can eliminate atheistic Communism for all time and usher in the millennium." Merton then remarked that he was no seer but that this attitude "may very well be the most diabolical of all illusions, the great and not even subtle temptation of a Christianity that has grown rich and comfortable and is satisfied with its riches."[1]

The real issue may turn out to be the issue of the haves vs. the have-nots. The compulsive way in which some choose to see in every area of civil unrest communist inspiration may be a way of America's evading responsibility as an affluent nation to come to grips with the plight of the poor in third world countries. This does not overlook the oppression and evil mania of Russian totalitarianism. It does say one has a responsibility before God of removing the "plank" from our eye (Lk. 6:41). Add to this the demonic illusion, which Jesus predicted, that in persecuting and even torturing people, they "will claim to be serving God" (Jn. 16:2). This is a special danger among church people and all Christians. Sometimes their anticommunism or their identification of God with country, or of God with "Western civilization" is so intense that they really do rationalize the most inhuman behavior toward those whom they believe to represent evil.

The seeds of similar responses are beginning to appear in America. Christians who protest certain policies of some multinationals are quickly labeled "naive," "unrealistic," "tools of the Marxists," "communists." Bishops are labeled "un-American," "softheaded," "liberals." Will torture find a place in America too—precisely under the guise of "national security"? Will similar patterns that have existed in Latin America develop in the United States? Repression causes reaction, and then greater repression is exercised to control the reaction that it created in the first place. Extremes arise gradually and are rarely perceived for what they are—extremes! The *right* creates the *left*. The *left* creates the *right*. The terrible irony is that in their anticommunist or antifascist hysteria people can become as repressive and as brutal as communism or fascism has been throughout its history. One takes on the enemy's evil.

Nonviolence as a Christian Dimension of Social Justice

During times when religious people become justice-oriented and feel the hatred and slander against them, we begin to understand how we must conduct ourselves. That is why I believe in the importance of avoiding an apocalyptic spirit. I mean that one must work nonviolently in every issue, and must be willing to undergo some nonsuccess—even some misunderstanding. A just social order will always be attained not according to our own timetable, or according to our own social project, but only in God's time. The spirit of Mahatma Gandhi hovers over the twentieth century, inviting us to penetrate the meaning of our own Jesus of Nazareth. Yet in proposing nonviolence one must guard against what Merton calls "mystification"—a form of passivity that is satisfied with the status quo. We have to realize that it may be a somewhat comfortable North American affluence that allows us to speak *easily* in behalf of nonviolence. One must judge slowly and with compassion those in desperate situations of oppression, who see no other way of survival except through what they feel is simply traditional application of just-war teaching. We need not necessarily agree with them but we can try to make sure that our own nonviolence is truly a strategy against oppression and injustice rather than the comfortable doctrine of those who sit on top of the world.

Another dimension of nonviolence has touched me in recent years. It is possible to talk and propose nonviolence in almost the same way as any other political system. Yet this is a contradiction. Raimundo Panikkar has written of pluralism as part of God's trinitarian reality and how we must be careful not to slip into an authoritarian or ideological imposition of nonviolence itself.[2] Jesus confounds any doctrinaire attitudes. The way to oppose evil, Panikkar says, is not by dialectically opposing it, but by "transforming, converting, convincing, evolving, contesting—and all this mainly from within, as leaven, as witness, as martyr."[3]

Graced Social Justice

This brings us to a final concern. It is a certain fear of the very term "social justice"! The term has been frequently used in religious circles of late. It is needed and it does serve to awaken us to the fact that American Christians are called to more than merely "charity"; that there are systems of evil that are unjust at their roots; and that in some cases Americans have some responsibility for those systems. But, that being said, a caution is desperately needed. "Social justice" is a term that non-Christians also use. Church people, as Pope John Paul II seems to be saying, must always have another dimension to their justice. We have to be wary of becoming just another advocacy group or just another lobby.

At times justice will demand that we foster and endorse a

union or that we truly speak in advocacy and lobby for the spiritual needs of the poor. But we must, as Christians, learn to do these things with a *difference*.

Justice, in the New Testament, always carries the memory of God's justice. And God's justice is more than merely ethical. It is a justice that itself justifies through the God-given gifts of love and reconciliation.

God's justice embodied in the Lord Jesus is tempered with love and mercy. God sent his Son Jesus, who justifies us by laying down his life, by undergoing our evil. "It is rare that anyone should lay down his life for a just man. . . . It is precisely in this that God proves His love for us; that while we were still sinners, Christ died for us" (Rom. 5:7–9).

Every Christian's work for justice must possess something of creative, justice-giving love. Unless we learn something of this divine mode, our work for justice may become as harsh and repressive as the injustice we struggle against. Again, this is the gift of a Gandhi and a Martin Luther King, who teach us that we must look into the eyes of the enemy, of the oppressor, of the general, of the corporate executive, and see there the spark of God. We must see the enemy as always more than an enemy; we must see one loved and redeemed by the blood of the Lord. In this way we shall be following the wise words of John Paul II and of Pedro Arrupe, who warn us that, while we may use some aspects of Marxist structural analysis, still we must avoid all forms of class hatred or, in fact, any form of hatred.

This does not mean one cannot call evil "evil." Nor does it mean an unrealistic refraining from passion, or from a healthy and godly indignation. There are real injustices and real perpetrators of injustice. There are real "enemies." What we cannot release ourselves from is the ongoing effort to try to love our enemies, even those among our brothers and sisters in the church. How can love and renewal within the church thrive unless there is real struggling over honest issues and real efforts to love those who set themselves against work for the poor and for peace?

This is a long process of purification for everyone. Each side grows. We try not to harden ourselves or harden our "enemy." It means struggling to participate in the grace of the cross, indeed in the mystery and the miracle of Christ's love for his enemies. "Father, forgive them for they know not what they do," Jesus said on the cross. In our work for justice we must share Jesus' creative Spirit and thus not only demand justice but even create justice in love.

The work of social justice in any area is always an awesome task, a great burden, and one that can be undertaken only in deep communion with Jesus the Lord, who pours out his powerful Spirit upon us. We can take a lesson from the Quakers, who often repeat the great moral demand imposed upon the Christian, "to speak the truth in love."

This is more than the ordinary connotation of social justice. It is social justice with love-mercy, a *graced* social justice. And a graced social justice is more than a virtue of non-Christians. It becomes a Christian spirituality.

Notes

Prologue: The Meaning of a New Social Spirituality

1. Augustine, *Confessions,* Bk. 11 (Edw. Pusey Translation, New York: Random House, 1949), p. 253.
2. Thomas Merton, *Conjectures of a Guilty Bystander* (New York: Doubleday, Image Edition, 1968), p. 156.

1. The Structure and the Spiritual

1. Cf. John XXIII, *Pacem in Terris,* art. 130.
2. Paul VI, *Populorum Progressio,* art. 42, in Joseph Gremillion, ed., *The Gospel of Peace and Justice* (Maryknoll, N.Y.: Orbis Books, 1976).

2. Global Awareness: A Spirituality for Worshiping in Spirit and Truth

1. Paul VI, *Octogesima Adveniens,* art. 44, in Gremillion, ed., *The Gospel of Peace and Justice.*
2. James McGinnis, *Bread and Justice* (New York: Paulist Press, 1979).

3. Bread-breaking and a Pastoral Care of the Milieu

1. *Pastoral Constitution on the Church in the Modern World,* art. 2, in Abbott and Gallagher, eds., *The Documents of Vatican II* (New York: Guild Press, 1966).
2. Ibid., art. 55.
3. Ibid., art. 30.
4. Paul VI, *Octogesima Adveniens,* art. 12, in Gremillion, ed., *The Gospel of Peace and Justice.*
5. James Wallis, "Hope Our Strongest Weapon," *Catholic Worker,* June 1978, p. 1.

4. Pope John Paul II and Social Concern: A Clarifying Note

1. John Paul II, "The Address of Pope John Paul II Opening Deliberations of the Third General Assembly of Latin American Bishops," par. 1.4, in *Origins,* February 8, 1979, p. 532.
2. John Paul II, "Building a Human Society," par. 5, in *Origins,* February 26, 1981, p. 591.
3. John Paul II, "Justice and the Land," par. 6, in *Origins,* March 12, 1981, p. 618.
4. John Paul II, "On Liberation Theology," General Audience Address, February 21, 1979, in *Origins,* March 8, 1979, p. 601.
5. John Paul II, "The Address of Pope John II Opening Deliberations of the Third General Assembly of Latin American Bishops," par. III.2, in *Origins,* February 8, 1979, p. 536.
6. Ibid.

5. Eucharist and a Spirituality for Justice

1. Paul VI, *Octogesima Adveniens,* art. 48, in Gremillion, ed., *The Gospel of Peace and Justice.*
2. Augustine, *City of God,* 10,6 (New York: The Fathers of the Church, Inc., 1952).
3. John Paul II, "The Address Opening Deliberations . . . of Latin American Bishops," par. III.3, in *Origins,* February 8, 1979, p. 536.
4. E.g., Kammer, Smith, et al., " 'Burn-Out'—Contemporary Dilemma for the Jesuit Social Activist," in *Studies in the Spirituality of Jesuits,* American Assistancy Seminar on Jesuit Spirituality, St. Louis, Mo., Vol. X, No. 1, January 1978.
5. Pedro Arrupe, "Marxism and Catechesis," *Catholic Mind,* October 1978, p. 44.
6. John Paul II, "The Address Opening Deliberations . . . of Latin American Bishops," par. I.4, in *Origins,* February 8, 1979, p. 532.

6. Ministry in the Church and Structural Concern for Justice

1. Barbara Ward Jackson, *The Angry Seventies,* A Study Paper Prepared at the Request of the Pontifical Commission Justice and Peace (Rome: Pontifical Commission Justice and Peace, 1971), p. 61.
2. Ibid., pp. 62–63.
3. Sister Elena Maltis, "Thomas Merton: Symbol and Synthesis of Contemporary Catholicism," *The Critic,* Spring 1977, p. 28.
4. Ibid., p. 30.

5. Thomas Merton, *Contemplation in the World of Action* (New York: Doubleday, Image Edition, 1973), p. 161.

6. "This Land Is Home to Me," A Pastoral Letter on Powerlessness in Appalachia by the Catholic Bishops of the Region, in David O'Brien and Thomas Shannon, eds., *Renewing the Earth: Catholic Documents on Peace, Justice and Liberation* (New York: Doubleday, Image Edition, 1977), p. 484.

7. Ibid., p. 489.

8. G. Cottier, et al., eds., *Église et Pauvreté* (Paris: Les Éditions du Cerf, 1965), p. 174, as cited in Gustavo Gutiérrez, *A Theology of Liberation* (Maryknoll, N.Y.: Orbis Books, 1973), p. 47.

9. *Pastoral Constitution on the Church in the Modern World,* art. 39, in Abbot and Gallagher, eds., *The Documents of Vatican II* (New York: Guild Press, 1966).

10. Paul VI, "Opening Address," 1974 World Synod of Bishops, in *Catholic Mind,* March 1975, p. 6.

11. Statement of the 1974 World Synod of Bishops "On Human Rights and Reconciliation," in *Catholic Mind,* March 1975, p. 51.

12. Gordon Zahn, as cited in Paul Hanly Furfey, *The Morality Gap* (New York: Macmillan, 1968), p. 13.

13. Furfey, *The Morality Gap,* p. 9.

14. Cf. National Conference of Catholic Bishops, "The Right to a Decent Home," pars. 76, 80; statement issued November 20, 1975.

7. Why Do Social Teachings Have Little Impact? A Reflection

1. National Conference of Catholic Bishops, "The Economy: Human Dimensions," statement issued November 20, 1975.

2. National Conference of Catholic Bishops, "The Right to a Decent Home," statement issued November 20, 1975, par. 70.

3. Ibid., par. 80.

4. Barbara Ward Jackson, *The Angry Seventies* (Rome: Pontifical Commission Justice and Peace, 1971), p. 61.

8. Social Justice and Abortion

1. Bernard Nathanson, "Second Thoughts on Abortion from the Doctor Who Led the Crusade for It," *Good Housekeeping,* March 1976, p. 131.

2. H. Richard Niebuhr, *The Responsible Self* (New York: Harper and Row, 1963), pp. 47-68 passim.

9. The Arms Race and the American Parish

1. *Pastoral Constitution on the Church in the Modern World,* art. 80, in Abbot and Gallagher, eds., *The Documents of Vatican II* (New York: Guild Press, 1966).

10. The Catholic Conscience Faces the Military Draft

1. Cf. "Registration and the Draft: Statement by the Administrative Board of the U.S. Catholic Conference," *Catholic Mind,* June 1980, p. 2.

2. Pius XII, "Allocution to Military Doctors," October 19, 1953 as cited in Joseph J. Fahey, *Peace, War and the Christian Conscience* (New York: Christopher pamphlet), p. 12. Also cited in Herbert Vorgrimler, ed., *Commentary on the Documents of Vatican II* (New York: Guild Press, 1966), p. 357.

3. John XXIII, *Pacem in Terris,* art. 127 (Boston: Daughters of St. Paul).

11. Disarmament in the Real World

1. James Dougherty, "Disarmament," *New Catholic Encyclopedia,* vol. 17, p. 189.

2. Charles McCarthy Interviewing Father George Zabelka, "I Was Told It Was Necessary," *Sojourners,* August 1980, pp. 12–15.

3. Figures are from Ruth Leger Sivard, *World Military and Social Expenditures* (Leesburg, Va.: World Priorities, 1979), p. 12.

12. Making the Connection between Sexual Ethics and Social Justice

1. Juan Luis Segundo, *The Liberation of Theology* (Maryknoll, N.Y.: Orbis Books, 1976), p. 9.

2. F. Tönnies, cited in Gregory Baum, *Religion and Alienation* (New York: Paulist Press, 1975), p. 49.

3. Midge Decter, "In Love with the New Sterility," *Catholic Mind,* September 1980, pp. 22–23.

4. Cf. Christopher Lasch, *The Culture of Narcissism* (New York: Warner Books, 1979), especially pp. 320–50.

13. Worship in Spirit and Truth—And Civil Religion

1. Will Herberg, *Protestant-Catholic-Jew* (New York: Doubleday, 1955), pp. 276–77.

2. Ibid., p. 227.

3. Ibid., pp. 279–80.

4. Marie Augusta Neal, *A Socio-Theology of Letting Go* (New York: Paulist Press, 1977).

5. Cf. José Comblin, *The Church and the National Security State* (Maryknoll, N.Y.: Orbis Books, 1979), pp. 79–98.

6. Robert Bellah, *The Broken Covenant* (New York: Seabury, 1975), p. 3.

7. H. Richard Niebuhr, *Christ and Culture* (New York: Harper and Row, 1951), p. 81.

8. John Paul II, *Redemptor Hominis,* art. 11, for reference to this theology.

9. Cf. Thomas Clark, "Societal Grace: For a New Pastoral Strategy," in *Soundings* (Washington, D.C.: Center of Concern, 1974), pp. 15–16. Cf. also "Public Policy and Christian Discernment," in Haughey, ed., *Personal Values in Public Policy* (New York: Paulist Press, 1979), pp. 212–29.

10. James Finley, *Merton's Palace of Nowhere* (Notre Dame, Ind.: Ave Maria Press, 1978), p. 52.

11. John Langan, "Liberation Theology in a Northern Context," *America,* January 27, 1979.

12. Jürgen Moltmann, "The American Dream," *Commonweal,* August 5, 1977, p. 491.

13. Ibid., p. 493.

Epilogue: The Growing Urgency

1. Thomas Merton, "The Roots of War," *The Catholic Worker,* June 1980, p. 5. The article was previously published in *The Catholic Worker,* October 1961.

2. Raimundo Panikkar, "The Myth of Pluralism: The Tower of Babel—A Meditation on Non-Violence," *Cross Currents,* Summer 1979, p. 223.

3. Ibid., p. 222.

Bibliography

The field is very wide. The bibliography could be immense. But in order to avoid paralyzing the reader, I have chosen to list those works which are written in a more popular style, or those which are representative of important perspectives or of an important author.

Social Spirituality

James Burtchaell. *Philemon's Problem*. Chicago: Acta Foundation, 1973.

Dom Helder Camara. *The Desert is Fertile*. Maryknoll, N.Y.: Orbis Books, 1974.

Thomas Clark, ed. *Above Every Name: The Lordship of Christ and Social Systems*. New York: Paulist Press, 1980.

Michael Crosby. *Spirituality of the Beatitudes*. Maryknoll, N.Y.: Orbis Books, 1981.

Dorothy Day. *The Long Loneliness*. New York: Harper and Row, originally published 1952; recently published with Introduction by Daniel Berrigan, 1981.

John Haughey, ed. *Personal Values and Public Policy*. New York: Paulist Press, 1979.

Joseph Holland and Peter Henriot. *Social Analysis: Linking Faith and Justice*. Washington, D.C.: Center of Concern, 1980.

David Hollenbach. *Claims in Conflict: Retrieving and Renewing the Catholic Human Rights Tradition*. New York: Paulist Press, 1979.

Thomas Merton. *Conjectures of a Guilty Bystander*. New York: Doubleday, Image Edition, 1968.

David O'Brien. *The Renewal of American Catholicism*. New York: Oxford University Press, 1972.

Global Justice and Spirituality-Theology

Pedro Arrupe. "Marxist Analysis by Christians." *Origins,* December 8, 1980.

Richard Barnet and Ronald Müller. *Global Reach: The Power of the Multinational Corporations.* New York: Simon and Schuster, 1974.

Willy Brandt, ed. *North-South.* The Report of the Independent Commission on International Development Issues under the Chairmanship of Willy Brandt. Cambridge, Mass.: The MIT Press, 1980.

Gustavo Gutiérrez. *A Theology of Liberation.* Maryknoll, N.Y.: Orbis Books, 1973.

Barbara Ward Jackson. *The Rich Nations and the Poor Nations.* New York: W. W. Norton and Co., 1962.

Penny Lernoux. *Cry of the People.* New York: Doubleday, 1980.

Richard McCormick. "The Church and Human Rights." *Catholic Mind,* November 1978.

James McGinnis. *Bread and Justice.* New York: Paulist Press, 1979.

Kathleen and James McGinnis. *Parenting for Peace and Justice.* Maryknoll, N.Y.: Orbis Books, 1981.

H. Richard Niebuhr. *Christ and Culture.* New York: Harper and Row, 1951.

Juan Luis Segundo. *The Hidden Motives of Pastoral Action.* Maryknoll, N.Y.: Orbis Books, 1978.

Spirituality and Peace

Daniel Berrigan. *Uncommon Prayer.* New York: Seabury Press, 1978.

Helen Caldicott. *Nuclear Madness: What You Can Do.* Brookline, Mass.: Autumn Press, 1978.

Chris Grannis, et al. *The Risk of the Cross: Christian Discipleship in the Nuclear Age.* New York: Seabury, 1981.

Richard McSorley. *The New Testament Basis of Peacemaking.* Washington, D.C.: Center for Peace Studies, Georgetown University, 1979.

Thomas Merton. *Faith and Violence.* Notre Dame: University of Notre Dame Press, 1968.

Thomas Merton. *Gandhi on Non-Violence.* New York: New Directions, 1964.

Raimundo Panikkar. "The Myth of Pluralism: The Tower of Babel—A Meditation on Non-Violence." *Cross Currents,* Summer 1979, pp. 197–230.

Thomas Shannon, ed. *War or Peace? The Search for New Answers.* Maryknoll, N.Y.: Orbis Books, 1980.

Gene Sharp. *The Politics of Non-Violent Action.* Boston: Porter Sargent Publisher, 1973.

Gordon Zahn. *In Solitary Witness—The Life and Death of Franz Jägerstätter.* Collegeville, Minn.: The Liturgical Press, 1978; original publication, 1964.

Gordon Zahn. *War, Conscience and Dissent.* New York: Hawthorne Press, 1967.

Connecting Abortion and Sexual Issues with Spirituality

James T. Burtchaell, ed. *Abortion Parley.* Mission, Kans.: Andrews and McMeel, 1980.

William Everett and T. J. Bachmeyer. *Disciplines in Transformation: A Guide to Theology and the Behavioral Sciences.* Washington, D.C.: University Press of America, 1979.

Rosemary Haughton. *The Passionate God.* New York: Paulist Press, 1981.

Christopher Lasch. *The Culture of Narcissism.* New York: Warner Books, 1979.

Francis X. Meehan. *Pro-Life Work and Social Justice.* NCCB Committee for Pro-Life Activities, Respect Life Series, Washington, D.C., 1980.

National Conference of Catholic Bishops, Committee for Pro-Life Activities, *Respect Life Booklet,* Washington, D.C., 1981-82.

John Noonan. *A Private Choice: Abortion in America in the Seventies.* New York: The Free Press, 1979.

"What Does It Mean to Be Pro-Life?" special issue of *Sojourners,* November 1980.

Sources for Official Documentation

For Papal and Synodal Statements see:

Joseph Gremillion, ed. *The Gospel of Peace and Justice.* Mary-knoll, N.Y.: Orbis Books, 1976.
David O'Brien and Thomas Shannon, eds. *Renewing the Earth: Catholic Documents on Peace, Justice and Liberation.* New York: Doubleday, Image Edition, 1977.

For statements of the National Conference of Catholic Bishops and of the United States Catholic Conference, see:

Brian Benestad and Francis Butler, eds., *Quest for Justice*, A Compendium of U.S. Bishops' Statements 1966–1980. (Washington, D.C.: NCCB, 1981).
Catholic Mind, America Press, New York.
Origins, 1312 Massachusetts Ave., Washington, D.C.

Resources for Action and Materials

Catholic Peace Fellowship
339 Lafayette St.
New York, NY 10012

Center for Peace Studies
Georgetown University
O'Gara Building
37th and 0 Sts. N.W.
Washington, DC 20057

Pro-Lifers for Survival
345 E. Ninth St.
Erie, PA 16503

Office of International Justice and Peace
United States Catholic Conference
1312 Massachusetts Ave. N.W.
Washington, DC 20005

Center of Concern
3700 13th St. N.E.
Washington, DC 20017

Interfaith Center for Corporate Responsibility
475 Riverside Drive
New York, NY 10115

Pax Christi
3000 N. Mango Ave.
Chicago, IL 60634

Overseas Development Council
1717 Massachusetts Ave. N.W.
Washington, DC 20036

Bread for the World
207 E. 16th St.
New York, NY 10003

NARMIC/AFSC
American Friends Service Committee
1501 Cherry St.
Philadelphia, PA 19102